It's easy to get lost in the shuffle. T[...]
longing to find our way back to Him[...]

—JENNIE ALLEN, founder, IF: Gath[...]

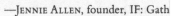

Sara's writing is exquisite. Her words remind us that nothing goes unnoticed by the God who delights in us.

—KATIE DAVIS MAJORS, author, *Kisses from Katie*

Listening in on Sara's conversations with God will call your heart, as it did mine, to want more time with Him.

—BARBARA RAINEY, FamilyLife; author, *Letters to My Daughters*

This book will prick your heart and encourage your soul. Let it rearrange your thinking in the most eternally beautiful of ways.

—KAREN EHMAN, speaker, Proverbs 31 Ministries; author, *Keep It Shut*

This book is exactly what my soul needed. Sara writes with profound wisdom and humble sincerity.

—SARAH MACKENZIE, author, *Teaching from Rest*

What a beautiful gift! *Unseen* invites us into the blessed center of what we were made for.

—CHRISTY NOCKELS, songwriter; *The Glorious in the Mundane* podcast

Sara exposes the beauty of abiding in the unseen and unrecognized, and we can't help but desire the same.

—RUTH CHOU SIMONS, author, *GraceLaced*; gracelaced.com

This journey into hiddenness will usher you to a place of newfound identity and intimacy with God.

—ALLEN ARNOLD, author, *The Story of With*

Sara winsomely models what we all desperately need: to long for the praise of God instead of craving the praise of man.

—DEE BRESTIN, author, *The Friendships of Women*

This book will inspire you to keep being faithful, to see beauty right where you are, and to rest in God's sweet love for you every day.

—SALLY CLARKSON, author, *The Lifegiving Home*; Sallyclarkson.com

With both wonder and practicality, *Unseen* will escort you to find that longed for place of joy and stability—hidden in His gaze.

—DANA CANDLER, author, *Deep unto Deep*

I'm desperate to "waste" more time with Jesus after reading *Unseen*, and I will recommend it over and over again.

—JEANNIE CUNNION, author, *Mom Set Free*

Sara shows us the power of wonder and stillness in the midst of crazy days. She gives us the courage to become unseen.

—SUSAN ALEXANDER YATES, speaker; author, *Risky Faith*

Because of this book, I have remembered who I truly am and what I truly desire. Sara's quiet story is transformative.

—CHRISTIE PURIFOY, author, *Roots and Sky*

You can't read this spectacular book without wanting more of Jesus, the one who always sees you right where you are.

—JENNIFER DUKES LEE, author, *The Happiness Dare*

Sara reminds us that being hidden with God is never time wasted. I desire a deeper friendship with God after reading her words.

—ESTHER FLEECE, author, *No More Faking Fine*

I will return to this beautiful and powerful book when I need a reminder of God's faithfulness, purposes, and love for me.

—AMY JULIA BECKER, author, *A Good and Perfect Gift*

Unseen is pregnant with the revelation that we can do nothing to earn God's love, a love we can experience when we are the least "useful" to him.

—SARA HALL, marathon runner; The Hall Steps Foundation

Sara turns our eyes to the beautiful reality that God is happily engaged in our everyday moments.

—CHRISTINE HOOVER, author, *Messy Beautiful Friendship*

If you are tugged by the allure of a life that makes a difference and are a bit disoriented by it all, *Unseen* is a must-read.

—RUTH SCHWENK, TheBetterMom.com; coauthor, *Pressing Pause*

UNSEEN

ALSO BY SARA HAGERTY

Every Bitter Thing Is Sweet:
Tasting the Goodness of God in All Things

UNSEEN

THE GIFT *of* BEING HIDDEN *in a* WORLD THAT LOVES *to be* NOTICED

SARA HAGERTY

ZONDERVAN

Unseen
Copyright © 2017 by Sara Hagerty

Requests for information should be addressed to:
Zondervan, *3900 Sparks Dr. SE, Grand Rapids, Michigan 49546*

ISBN 978-0-310-35837-4 (softcover)

ISBN 978-0-310-35053-8 (audio)

ISBN 978-0-310-33998-4 (ebook)

Published in association with Yates and Yates, www.yates2.com.

Cover design: James W. Hall IV
Cover photo: Shutterstock®
Interior design: Sarah Johnson and Kait Lamphere

Printed in the United States of America

19 20 21 22 23 24 25 26 27 28 29 /LSC/ 15 14 13 12 11 10 9 8 7 6 5 4 3 2 1

TO CLAIRE

*Your life gave dignity to hiddenness long
before I knew what it was.
Until we meet again.*

CONTENTS

FOREWORD

My wife, Alyssa, and I were born toward the end of the 1980s. We grew up in the 1990s and early 2000s. 'N Sync, breakaway pants, yo-yos, chia pets—this was us.

Another byproduct of being born at this time is that we are among the first native users of the internet. We don't remember a time before it existed. I recall being ten years old and getting AOL dialup for the first time and using AOL instant messenger to chat with all my friends.

The internet is one of those things that's both a blessing and a curse—a blessing, because of the sheer power of its innovation and how it has given access to information and given voice to so many who never had one, but a curse because it's creating a new humanity, a new way of doing things, rewiring our being.

We are shifting the way we live in order to create better pictures to post and content to create. Many of us no longer go on a hike and then take a picture to remember it. We want to take a picture to post, so we go on a hike to get that picture. It's *driving* us. It's feeding our insatiable desire to be seen. Be affirmed. Be noticed. Be loved. Be liked.

A few years ago in our home state of Washington, a guy

wanted to get a selfie with a moving train in the background. He wasn't paying attention to the track he was standing on, and another train sped right into him, killing him instantly.

And this isn't an anomaly. An entire Wikipedia page is devoted to selfie-related injuries and deaths. We are, literally, dying to be seen.

But what if there's a better way? What if we can find joy and affirmation in the hidden, the quiet, and the mundane?

Because that's exactly where Jesus says it's at. There's holy in the mundane. There's grace in taking out the trash. There's blessing in the thirty-year office job.

Why?

Because one thing we don't celebrate much these days, one thing Jesus clearly does celebrate, is faithfulness. Consistency. Obscurity.

When I was having coffee with a friend recently, he mentioned getting invited to a man retreat in the mountains, where they would shoot guns, cook meat, and pursue God. He admitted that God has shown up and transformed a lot of the guys who have gone in the past. But he said he didn't think he should go.

I asked why, and he said, "Because staying here and meeting with my mentor once a week for the next five years is harder, and that's what I think I should do instead." He was aware enough to know that for him, the retreat would be just a mountaintop experience. Sure, when he came back, he'd have something to show for it, but God was calling him to the unseen, to the unnoticed.

And that's what a lot of us are missing. We are trying to

get the top-ramen, two-ingredient, sixty-second Jesus when the long game is where it's happening. A tree doesn't look like it's growing if you stare at it every single day. But if you water it, prune it, and take care of it, and every year compare it with the way it looked the year before, you'll see that all the growth happened in hiddenness.

When you walk with Jesus, the hiddenness is where you are seen the most. By Him. With ferocious, white-hot, piercing eyes. And his gaze of love is what changes us, what makes us, what we all are desperately searching for in the first place.

And that's why this book is so important, why we are so thankful for Sara. Not many people are shouting this message from the mountaintops, because not a lot of people have found this secret, but Sara has, and her story is compelling and inspiring. It changed us, and I know it will change you.

We are dying to be seen, but the good news is we can know we are already seen by the one who matters the most—Jesus.

—*Jeff and Alyssa Bethke*

one

BEAUTIFUL WASTE

Opening Our Eyes to the Unseen

"Jesus came to Bethany."
—JOHN 12:1

I graduated from college unwaveringly convinced: I would change the world for God. As a college student, I volunteered with a high school ministry, sharing the gospel with hardened-to-Christ teenagers. And I was all in. When I wasn't studying, I spent time with students in their world. The deepest of time, one life pouring into another. I became addicted to seeing God influence the most unsuspecting lives.

The year I left college, I joined the high school ministry as full-time staff. I was on fire for God and ravenous to see what He could do. I believed there is no higher calling than to be used by God to love the lost. It was a belief that fueled me but also made me feel as if I were somehow critical to God's work. And in subtly assenting to this understanding of my role, I exchanged compassion for judgment of others who were going to waste their twenties on anything I deemed to be of lesser eternal value. After all, wasn't my work helping God change lives most important? I was filled with ambition.

The annual highlight of our ministry was the week we took a bus full of living-loud adolescents to camp. Every activity and experience was beautifully designed to illustrate the person and love of Jesus to our high school students. Outdoor adventures each day bled into evenings of sharing the gospel. We told the story of Jesus and gave teenagers the opportunity to invite Him into their stories. And many of them did. On the last night of camp, those who had decided to follow Jesus were given the chance to stand up and announce this life shift.

That final night was what I looked forward to all week long. It often remained suspended in my memory throughout the year like flakes in a snow globe: distant, dazzling, majestic. A few hundred sweaty teenagers who'd just spent their last hours at camp cramming dirty laundry into overstuffed suitcases, cleaning out bunks, and saying the kind of tearful goodbyes you typically say to lifelong friends, despite the fact that they'd met them just seven days before, gathered in the clubhouse. The room swelled with people and music and anticipation and new lives.

When the music was over and the final talk concluded, nervous varsity basketball players and homecoming queens and kids in the math club each stood up one at a time and shared that this week they'd given their lives to Jesus. "Let the redeemed of the Lord say so" (Ps. 107:2 ESV).

My heart raced on those nights because I knew it was just the beginning. I knew the bigger impact those dozens of yeses would have. In the year ahead, some of those teenagers in the room would open their Bibles for the first time ever and ask God to invade the world around them. Their changed lives would ripple out to influence families, friends, and football teams. Some would tell their children and their children's children that this was the night that changed everything. I looked around the room and tried to take it all in, as if my panoramic perspective could absorb the magnitude of such a night, of such a week. Reflected in the flushed faces of teenagers who wanted a fresh start, who wanted Jesus, I saw the face of God.

After camp was over, I came home to an even longer list of lives I wanted to influence. When teenagers are "on fire" for Jesus, their unchurched parents start showing up to church on Sunday, asking questions, and joining Bible studies. It was what I'd prayed for. It was everything I'd wanted when I started in full-time ministry. The work was sometimes hard and often exhausting, but the life-changing stories fueled me. They validated my calling and my passion. They kept me in it.

Until one year they didn't.

Lives around me were changing for Jesus, but my life had grown stagnant. My passion for ministry waned and a vague emptiness took its place. I'd have dinner with a teenager who'd just asked Jesus into her heart and find myself mindlessly repeating answers I'd said for years. I knew how to share about God's love with others, but I no longer felt like I was living in it myself. There was a voice in my head that wondered, *Am I just saying these things about God, or do I really believe them?*

So I'd come home and check in on my heart, carving out space to sit with God and ask that question out loud. Except when I got there, that space and time alone with Him felt awkward, like I was supposed to share the kinds of things you say mostly only in hushed tones to a close friend, but instead this was a conversation with a distant acquaintance. I didn't quite know how or where to start. More than thirty minutes with my Bible open, but without a Bible study to plan, and I didn't know who I was supposed to be. I wasn't sure who God was either, in my less productive quiet time and in the "nonessential" moments of life.

I knew Jesus as the one who'd walked on water and calmed the storm and healed a leper. I could describe that God in my sleep. But who was God to me during those ordinary days, the days when I didn't need Him to calm a storm or walk across the water or help me plan a Bible study? What about the days when I had to pay bills and clean the toilet and babysit a friend's children? I had no doubt He was the God of hardened teenagers, warming their cold hearts and drawing them closer into Himself. I knew He was the God of people who devoted themselves to ministry, to constant relationship with others, to speaking and leading. But who was He to me when I wasn't changing the world? When I was by myself? Who was He to me when I had nothing at all to give Him?

These questions would eventually guide my eyes to the unseen beauty of a hidden life in God. But as it is with most beginnings, first they were unnerving. I knew God was benevolently disposed toward me, but I'd always assumed His benevolence was also connected to my producing something for His kingdom. When I felt productive in ministry, it wasn't hard to imagine that God had loving thoughts toward me or that He looked at me with warm affection. I had a harder time trying to imagine what He might be thinking about me during the hours of the day when I wasn't doing anything tangible for Him—the hours of the day when I felt naked and exposed, unable to hide behind my productivity for the kingdom of God. What was the expression on His face when I didn't have a trail of changed lives behind mine? How did He feel about me on Saturday morning while I was lying on the couch in sweatpants, exhausted from the week?

But something inside of me knew there had to be more to my life with God than being productive and sharing the good news with others. Something inside of me craved the God I'd find when I wasn't changing the world. I'd always thought my craving for more in life would be satisfied with more ministry, more impact, more good works for God. But instead of filling me with more, the escalating effort I put into those things slowly left me feeling empty.

As I saw it, I gave in to burnout, but there was more to it than that. I'd been driven by a passion to see lives change, but I also craved the validation I received when my life made a notable impact on someone else's. Over time, the deep satisfaction I'd found in my work lessened. The nagging drive, albeit subtle, to which I'd responded to do more and more continued to leave me feeling inadequate. My expectations for myself increased as my ability to meet those expectations diminished. Even worse, I began to see myself as critical to God's success. But I just couldn't do it anymore.

So I left the ministry I admired.

I, the fiery-eyed, will-not-waste-my-life poster child, succumbed.

I took a break from telling others about Jesus and found a part-time job. For well into a year, I spent my afternoons amid bouquets of imported French lavender, handcrafted soaps, and Italian pottery at a boutique. I was instructed *not* to dust the porcelain guinea hens or stacks of plates—people feel at home in cottage dust, apparently—and sometimes I banked no more than five transactions in a day. Mine had become the wasted life I once judged, the person who ended most days without a single story of kingdom impact or even a spiritual conversation. Instead of raising money to dig wells for people without clean water, I spent my hours among decorative water pitchers priced at one hundred dollars a pop. It was a life I swore I'd never have—unproductive. A colossal waste of my time, energy, and gifts.

But to the surprise of my productivity-oriented heart, that quiet little storefront in the Barracks Road Shopping Center became a place where I met God.

I brought my Bible to work and cracked it open as I sat behind the register. I had hours unplanned for one of the first times in my life. I talked through God's Word with Him, and I did so slowly—less extrapolating a lesson and more absorbing who the person was within those stories. I circled the pottery-stacked farm tables with it, praying one passage at a time while the smells of French-milled soaps wafted in the air. And as I did so, I noticed things about Jesus I'd never seen while preparing to teach a Bible study or codifying a set of verses into a single palatable point. I was noticing more of Him as I read, and realizing that He too was seeing me in the minutia of my day. I was seeing the shape of the person who *was* this Word that I'd memorized and quoted for years.

He had eyes and a face.

His hands held a hammer, washed feet, cupped the faces of children. And adults.

He sweated.

I discovered layers of God's nature I hadn't considered when I was barreling through life, when He was only a leader and a coach to me. Slowly, my desire to see and feel who He is within the pages of His Word prompted me to look at the lines on His face. To take a long and thoughtful look at Him, and not just once. As I did so, I saw not only that He invited me to see Him—in the minutia of stories I'd read for years to gain broad themes and lessons—but also that He also saw me, right there in my middle minutes. For perhaps one of the first times in my life, I made eye contact with God.

His life on the earth and in these pages held a facial expression. Toward me. When I slowed, I saw that He too looked past my complexities to know and respond to my heart. He wasn't driving me to produce in such a way that all I saw was the back of His shoulders and His firm gait as He charged ahead of me; He was turned toward me and looking into me with a softheartedness and an ever-unfolding open stance.

His face held a gentle expression. *Loving* expression. Toward me, who was doing nothing for Him.

Just as little children need to be seen, need to see their reflection in the eyes of a loving parent, I needed to see God seeing me as I spent hours in the stillness of that store. I needed to see the twinkle in His eyes when He looked at me. I'd lived most of my Christian life in deficit, not seeing that spark and imagining His eyes to be dull and hardened toward me. I needed to know what He thought of me in my unproductivity, when I was doing nothing to advance His kingdom, just paying my bills, buying groceries, and making the bed. If God had tender thoughts toward me in my mundane moments, then those were moments in which I wanted to encounter Him. I wanted to believe that the same God who was pleased with me when I shared the gospel still smiled when I took out the trash or took a nap. If I could meet God's eyes in all those ordinary times—if I could just see the spark, there—then my assumptions about what matters most to God would have to change.

And I wanted them to change.

In a year that felt like failure by all my ministry productivity standards, I grew desperate to lock eyes with God and see His real expression toward me. I knew if on an average Tuesday afternoon I could see God as the Initiator, the one who gently draws me close and with tenderness, then I could finally find deep soul-rest. I wouldn't have to work so hard to get God's attention, because I already had it. Every single ordinary minute of my day would be an opportunity to encounter God's unwavering gaze.

This is hiddenness. It's not a natural concept for our human minds to apprehend. There are times when God tucks us away. He might hide us in a difficult job or an unwelcomed circumstance where we feel like no one gets us, where we feel misunderstood. He might hide us in a crowd where we feel lost—unseen—or behind the front door of our homes, changing diapers and burping babies. He does this all so that we might see another side of Him, this God who looks deeply and knowingly into us when no one else is looking or noticing, and come alive under that eye.

Sure, this hiddenness may feel undesirable at first. We resist it. We want out of the dead-end job and to be done with the ministry or church where we're not properly acknowledged for who we are and what we do. (And most of our friends might counsel us to do that, to get out.) We want to climb out from underneath burp cloths and laundry and serving in silence into a world where someone notices, where we're not only seen but appreciated, validated by those around us.

And yet even as we might naturally clamor to get out of these places, He continues to use the unwelcomed, unbending circumstances to show us that He sees, He knows—yes, even in this job we're praying desperately to be able to leave or this church that feels as if its people haven't yet discovered our capabilities. We feel like we're waiting it out or merely enduring hardship, but, from God's angle, these times are purposed.

In the words of Paul, these hidden times allure us to "think about the things of heaven, not the things of earth" (Col. 3:2).

In no way do we naturally fall into this way of thinking. We breathe and pay our bills and use our words, all in the temporal. We need help to look at the unseen, the things of heaven, not the things we can touch with our hands or gauge with a measuring stick. Our truest lives—once we come to know Him—don't reside in the temporal world. Hiddenness is God's way of helping us with this holy detachment, slowly releasing our clutch on "the things of earth," which we were never intended to grip.

Paul goes on to say, "For you died to this life, and your real life is hidden with Christ in God" (Col. 3:3 NLT).

It was in that cottage boutique—during a time when I also felt that I was experiencing the death of my dreams—that I first tasted this hiddenness. That's when I first practiced "wasting time with God." Up to that point, spending twenty to thirty minutes in the morning with God—my Bible and journal open on my lap—was all I needed and all I could justify. I'd never considered setting aside more time to spend with God. I'm certain I subconsciously saw that extra time to be wasteful, discarding otherwise productive hours and disguising sloth. But as my heart was resuscitated behind the storefront window, I started to see the worth of searching Him out in these undocumented, unproductive hours. And so I cautiously started to give Him access to the parts of me that no one, including myself, had seen before.

As my heart ebbed from a flurried life into the quiet of that store, the buried parts of my thinking surfaced. One day, the wife of one of my husband's college friends came into the boutique to browse. Instead of being excited to see her, I felt a flash-rush of unexpected shame. She'd caught me being insignificant—not sharing the gospel, not advancing the kingdom of God, not using my college degree, but selling pricey tablecloths—and I suddenly felt the need to justify my dormant existence.

No sooner had the glass door shut behind her than an urge to quit this job and do something significant with my life consumed my thinking.

In years past, I would have obsessed about that thought for days and weeks, but in the quiet of that store and the quieting of my activity, I was less threatened and more curious. Time and a newly tender brush with God created a safe space for me to see the layers within me. Initially after our twelve-minute exchange, she seemed successful and I felt foolishly stuck. She had real accomplishments to share, and I knew how to order her the correct color of tablecloth she wanted from our sister store. But I soon realized that the urge to quit that overtook me the minute she left wasn't one to guide me. Instead, it was an indicator of a deeper question I needed to ask of God: *How do You see me, especially now when I feel unproductive and unsuccessful? How do You see me when I feel naked without my life's impact to hide behind?*

These were the things that surfaced in the hours when I was on the clock but not changing lives. I started a new dialogue with God that didn't include a plea for Him to use me in someone else's life or to make my life matter. It was a conversation in which I saw that He cared for the inner workings of my heart. He cared about the insecurities that plagued me. I felt the pulse of His life in the biblical stories for which I had lost my passion. Not even whole sentences but mere phrases from His Word that had once been pat answers were transformed into poetry, renewing my mind and sparking fresh and intimate conversations with God. Not only was He becoming more real to me as I took time not just to study but to soak in Scripture, He was becoming personal. To me.

This age-old God was newly vibrant to me. And I was starting to think He might actually like me, right there in that store, where I was getting paid just above minimum wage and not using my college degree.

In the pages of His Word, I saw Him validate the hearts of those who sought Him in secret. God said to Samuel, "For the LORD does not see as man sees; for man looks at the outward appearance, but the LORD looks at the heart" (1 Sam. 16:7). I heard Him whisper those same words to me. I wanted to shame myself, and yet I felt oddly seen and known and enjoyed by God, simply because I had turned my heart and my conversation to Him in that moment.

Years before, I never could have believed that God would enjoy me in that state—or even tolerate me. But when the store was empty and the sun was fading, aslant on the floor amid farm tables stacked with overpriced tablecloths, I locked eyes with God anew. I sensed His pleasure. I was wasting time with God.

God liked me.

And He wanted to spend time with me.

When you're with someone who knows the quirks of your heart and enjoys you anyway, it's only natural that you want to spend more time with that person. When God was attentive to me—even the small, unseen parts of me—I wanted to reciprocate. I wanted to sit with Him and study the lines and contours of His face.

I was beginning to believe that maybe who I was in secret

was reason for praise. Maybe my unproductive, looking-up-at-Him life produced awe among the angels.

Now I was no longer unsticking the pages of my Bible out of obligation. Instead, I was driven by a desire to see and know more of God. In every passage, in every verse, I was clawing my way into what was life to me: the delight on God's face turned toward me. I'd been fiercely searching the crowd for that face for years, thinking I would find it only in the praise or approval among the masses, in the eyes of other people. But now I could see it manifest in God's face. God delighted in me even when I felt I least deserved it.

God was growing me, in secret, tucked well behind the display window in a Barracks Road boutique.

Rarely do I notice the roots of a tree unless my feet stumble over them. I may notice the way branches above me cut across the sky as I pull out of my driveway. I may sit with my toddler in the shade or pick apples at an orchard with my children in early autumn. I may roll a newly fallen leaf between my fingers. But most of the time I walk unaware right over the roots, the hidden life of every tree that makes everything else—branches, shade, fruit, and leaves—possible at all.

Often the obvious accomplishments of our days get most of our attention. Noticing the roots, much less tending to them, seems secondary when there are branches to climb and fruit to pick. We live for what is right in front of us, while God is ever so gently calling us toward the unseen. His unseen.

We come alive in the unseen.

We were made for it.

We are formed in it.

I'd spent most of my twenties with a similar lack of awareness in my relationship with God. I envisioned growth to be outstretched branches—majestic when hit by the sun and seen against the pure blue sky—and mostly ignored the roots. But I could no longer grow tall in God without caring for my root system, without acknowledging that something buried beneath the surface gives life to the trunk and branches I showed the world. Noticing and tending to my roots—my inner and hidden life with God—seemed secondary when there were important ministry branches to climb and spiritual fruit to produce and pick. But God was ever so gently inviting me back to the soil. To hide in Him rather than perform for Him, to shift my attention from branches to roots, from my visible work *for* God to my unseen life *in* God.

It was as if He was patiently drawing my eyes away from the branches and down to my thirsty roots. *You don't have to try so hard to leave your mark on the world, Sara. Come back to the soil. Leave your mark on Me.* This was the whisper from God that emerged in that unproductive season. *Spend, pour out, right here, and I'll grow the tree.*

I hadn't before considered that I could pour out my life at His feet, caring only for what He thought of me. This was beautiful waste.

I was moving from merely a God-*follower* to a God-*lover* when I noticed Him seeing me and knowing me in the middle minutes of my day and enjoying me, right there. Squandering time with God in the hidden place was turning me into one who would do anything to bring Him glory on the earth. What I forged with God in secret led to a sweet partnership with Him, the kind of partnership that leads any of us into great impact in this world—not because of the magnitude of what we do or how we feel when we're doing it but because of who He is to us.

Those hidden exchanges with Him began to fuel how I interacted with the world around me.

We were made to be seen—to have our baby hair clipped and saved, to have our milestones noticed, to be celebrated. But at the end of almost every well-intentioned baby book you'll probably find the blank pages. Eventually, no one has time to count the number of our teeth or of the new words we've learned. As we grow, we swirl in a sea of other faces, other ambitions. We might feel we're drowning in lost moments, unseen for who we are and who we could be. We might feel that parts of our lives are wasted.

The craving to be seen is universal: we were made to be known. But there is only one who can know us. He is the one who created us to live with moments and hours that no one else can understand.

And that's where the mysterious beauty of hiddenness comes in. We who live most of our days in and around the people of this world don't naturally hide ourselves in God. We don't naturally look to His expression toward us to drive us.

We respond instead to the looks and applause and the direction of others around us. Thus, He hides us. And masterfully.

Like He did with me, God sometimes hides us in obscure circumstances. He takes us out of an up-front role so we can discover the beauty of falling in love with Him when no one else is looking on or applauding. We sit behind a desk, toiling at a job no one appreciates. We push a stroller, change diapers, and rock crying babies to sleep. We work behind the scenes, clipboard in hand, serving the person on stage. We attend a church whose mission isn't the perfect fit with who we are and how we're gifted, and we serve, quietly and unacknowledged, in the background.

Sometimes God hides us in hardship or suffering. We limp through a broken marriage, wondering if life will ever mend. We get a late-night phone call and a tragedy forever splits our life into a before and an after. We lose our routine to a flurry of appointments with pediatric specialists and settle in for another long night at the hospital holding our child's hand.

Other times, God hides us in plain sight, right in the midst of a life that keeps going full tilt, so we learn how to find Him while pursuing a career or leading a ministry or running a household. We earn a doctorate degree, each letter behind our name representing long hidden hours, undocumented measures of hard work, and sacrifices that no one will fully know. We cheer on our children from the sidelines, knowing there is so much more to their story than the goals they've scored this season. We carry great responsibility at work or heading up a foundation, wearing a title that brings burdens few recognize or understand.

Yes, *all* of us world-changers, made by God for His glory, experience being hidden, hidden on purpose. Perhaps hidden for now simply because God enjoys how we give our all to Him—our thoughts, our prayers, our focused devotion—in private. (Would that be enough, to simply pour ourselves out for Him alone?)

We spend the majority of our lives hidden from others. Our secret thoughts, our sleep, our parenting and driving and grocery shopping. God designed us to hide in Him, not perform for Him.

In my early twenties, I was hidden in a boutique among antique farm tables stacked with table linens and pottery while my ministry dreams languished in a worn journal somewhere in the basement at home.

As a young married woman, I was hidden behind a desk when the guy who had an MBA took credit for months of my work and never gave me a nod or a second thought.

Years later, I was hidden, childless, at baby showers in a room full of women swapping birthing stories and maternity clothes.

I was hidden under mounds of paperwork and the debt of adoption as my friends nursed their babies.

I was hidden in a guest home in Ethiopia with a newly adopted child who cried for hours, and realized that none of my friends back home would ever understand the sweat I'd shed in just a few days of motherhood.

I was hidden holding that same child as he cried anew over wounds from living abandoned for too many years, years I could not reach back and heal.

I was hidden when I stood jittery behind a podium to tell my story, opening vulnerable parts of my life to scrutiny and criticism, and giving others opportunity to comment and misunderstand.

Most recently, I am hidden in sweatpants at home with six children, children whose needs render my days a forgettable blur unless I document them online. I am hidden when I sit alone at the end of these days, too exhausted even to fold laundry or help little fingers hold a crayon.

There was a time I lumped all of these experiences together and labeled them unproductive. Wasted and lost. But now I see them differently. These are paramount days, the most important ones, each filled with hours in which I can choose to hide myself in God.

And I join throngs of other women and men placed purposefully in hiding, who are also in training to be passionate lovers of God. They are cleaning toilets, punching time cards, changing bedpans, fielding criticism, and battling fatigue. With the opportunity to find Him in the midst of it all. No moment is too small, too insignificant to hide in God and waste time with Him.

God loves to hide us. Behind circumstances and callings and misjudgments and scorn from even the dearest of friends, He hides us. We may feel veiled and unnoticed, but God is training us to turn our eyes toward Him, to find Him there.

Our hidden places aren't signs of God's displeasure or punishment. The psalmist says that the one "who dwells in the secret place of the Most High" has a refuge and a fortress in God (Ps. 91:1). God doesn't banish us to this hidden place.

He *invites* us. And finding God in the secret can teach a heart to sing.

Mary of Bethany.

Jesus said of her, "Wherever this gospel is preached in the whole word, what this woman has done will also be told as a memorial to her" (Mark 14:9).

She may not be one of the few we memorialize in the gospels or among Jesus' followers. In her lifetime, she likely wasn't a gregarious ministry leader who attracted a large following.

She simply touched one life.

And then her story was told. Forever.

When Jesus came to Bethany six days before Passover, He walked into the mundane swirl of Mary's world—the roads her calloused and tired feet knew by memory, the place she fetched water, the floors she swept. And it was in the familiar and ordinary that something extraordinary happened. An extraordinary waste.

As Jesus dined with his friends, Mary poured perfume on His feet and then wiped them dry with her hair. Though others were scandalized and quick to criticize her actions, Jesus dignified her with His words. The Son of God was grateful for what this woman did. He even said that she would be known and highly regarded for her wastefulness.

Hers was the story He came to tell that night.

And it's true. More than two thousand years later, we know Mary not because of the food she may have served earlier in the day, the elderly relative she may have cared for, or even the prayers she may have offered. We know her because of her reckless, loving extravagance for God. And yet this public display of affection was also a hidden one. Hidden not because no one else was watching but because no one else really mattered.

Mary had eyes for one. Her motives were oriented toward Him. She wasn't driven to His feet by accolades, and she stayed despite criticism. What she cultivated with this man, Jesus, in the quiet and ordinary became her greatest expression.

This is radical love, according to Jesus.

In Mary, we see what it means to waste ourselves on God. In situations we might otherwise avoid or resent—the fourth-floor cubicle, the back row of singers, the laundry room—God invites us, through Mary's forever retold story, into an expression of radical love. The kind of unhinged love that lays everything at His feet whether or not anyone else ever sees, approves, or applauds.

The pieces of Mary's wasteful moment are a prism through which to consider this idea of hiddenness. God used a moment meant for God alone to invite others to Him. A moment in which she lived out no desire for acclaim and no fear of others' opinions. A moment, rooted in dozens of others before it, when Mary's love for and devotion to Jesus fueled what she performed.

In the chapters ahead, we'll explore the rich, yet often buried, opportunities God gives us in our own moments of hiddenness and just how to lean in, there, with expectation. And to grow. Deep. *Continually.*

This invitation to embrace hiddenness grows from a seasonal, one-time invitation into the question of our lives: *When no one else applauds you, when life is hard and makes no sense or simply feels like drudgery in the still quiet, will you hide yourself in Me? Will you waste your love on Me, here?*

———————— *For Your Continued Pursuit* ————————

1 Samuel 16:7 | Psalm 17:8 | Psalm 18:19 | Psalm 91:1 | Psalm 107:2 | Psalm 119:130 | Psalm 139 | Proverbs 25:2 | Song of Songs 2:14 | Isaiah 64:4 | Matthew 6:1–4 | Matthew 26:6–13 | Mark 14:9 | John 1:47–50 | 2 Corinthians 4:16–18 | Galatians 1:10 | Ephesians 3:17–19 | Philippians 1:6 | Colossians 3:1–4 | Hebrews 12:2

This section at the end of each chapter is for readers who, like me, want to dig deeper by tracing the teaching back to God's truth. Some verses are cited within each chapter and others are alluded to. I invite you to use these passages as starting points for hiding in God, for wasting time adoring Him, and for making His Word part of your everyday language.

two

Seen and Celebrated

Discovering Who We Are Apart from What We Do

"And Martha served."
—John 12:2

I was seventeen and still a baby in my faith when, in a flurry of opportunity and impulse, I got on a plane for the very first time and flew to a Christian camp in the Adirondack Mountains to wait tables for free.

I'd never been away from home for longer than a week. I was the kid who still got homesick during slumber parties just a year or two before. And I grumbled when my mom asked me to vacuum. Yet there I was, flying several states away to serve others from seven in the morning until ten at night for a month.

Our work crew (thirty of us high school volunteers) set tables, served plates, and cleaned up at breakfast, lunch, and dinner for three hundred loud, ravenously hungry peers every day. We raced from one meal to the next, barely catching our breath. Lunch crumbs were still under our fingernails when the dinner bell rang.

The work was taxing, but what hangs out in my memories are the pranks we played in the thirty minutes before bed, the dances we choreographed while cleaning up lunch, and the ten-minute make-a-best-friend-out-of-you conversations with people I've now called the dearest of friends for more than twenty years.

Somewhere between the hard work, late nights, and crazy pranks, our work crew leaders also had us memorizing Scripture. The first verse we memorized upon arriving at camp was this: "For even the Son of Man did not come to be served, but to serve, and to give His life a ransom for many" (Mark 10:45).

This verse was new to me. I hadn't known that service was part of the whole Jesus deal I'd signed up for—that it was His very life witness—until I memorized that verse. But that summer I got a preview of what it means to lay down my life. I also have a photo album full of pictures of celebrated moments with thirty other people. We weren't exactly suffering that month, and we certainly weren't doing everything in secret, but I was getting a gentle first taste of service.

At the time, service, much less *hidden* service—the kind Jesus offered when He washed the soil-stained feet of His disciples—had little appeal to me. It didn't need to. In this early stage of my relationship with God, everything felt flashy and fun and new. I wasn't inclined to give much thought to the less glamorous verses of the Bible.

Instead, I had a way of reframing Scripture to fit what made sense to me. I read, "Whoever wants to become great among you must be your servant. And whoever wants to be first must be your slave" (Matt. 20:26–27 NIV). Now, I could have seen this verse as an invitation, a way to experience His best intentions for me by serving. However, when the sixteen-year-old version of me reframed it, I understood it to say something like this: *Buck up and serve. We're called to hang out in the lowest places.*

Back then I read, "The greatest among you will be your servant. For those who exalt themselves will be humbled, and those who humble themselves will be exalted" (Matt. 23:11–12 NIV). And I reframed it, *Stifle desires to do anything for yourself. Serving is the best thing to do and the only thing that really matters.*

But there was a clanging dissonance between my longing to be noticed and the messages I received that seemed to teach these desires were wrong. To reconcile my understanding of service with my desires for acclaim and acknowledgment (desires that weren't a byproduct of being sixteen and immature but were inherent in me before and after adolescence), I stifled my desires. I shoved them deep inside and came to loathe that part of me that wanted to be noticed. I felt disgusted by any part of me that didn't line up with my reframed understanding of what it means to serve. It didn't occur to me to ask myself, *Could it be that God has made me with a desire to be seen and to be celebrated, but my desires are merely misplaced?*

The truth is we are made by God to be seen and celebrated. We like to hear our own names. When we're noticed and affirmed for our accomplishments or character traits, we feel that internal sigh of satisfaction that says, *Yes, I matter. To someone.* It's God who gives us this craving to be known, to realize that we do matter. Author and pastor Dallas Willard says it this way: "Unlike egotism, the drive to significance is a simple extension of the creative impulse of God that gave us being. . . . We were built to count, as water is made to run downhill. We are placed in a specific context to count in ways that no one else does. That is our destiny."[1]

We mattered before anyone else knew us, before we even had breath. David knew this: "For You formed my inward parts; You covered me in my mother's womb" (Ps. 139:13). We were conceived and we grew in hiddenness: "My frame was not hidden from You, when I was made in secret, and skillfully wrought in the lowest parts of the earth" (v. 15). Yet even in our natal hiddenness, we had a set of eyes on us. We lived for that one set of eyes: "Your eyes saw my substance, being yet unformed" (v. 16).

From the moment we were created, we were seen. And it was marvelous. Even before we had words, our souls were encoded to know God's image: "I will praise You, for I am fearfully and wonderfully made; marvelous are Your works, and that my soul knows very well" (v. 14).

The one whose hands formed the intricately pieced-together parts of us also had thoughts while He worked. David marveled, "How precious also are Your thoughts to me, O God!" (v. 17). Many thoughts: "How great is the sum of them! If I should count them, they would be more in number than the sand" (vv. 17–18). And God doesn't stop thinking about us. He never stops looking at and into us. There is never a time when we are unseen by Him: "Where can I go from Your Spirit? Or where can I flee from Your presence?" (v. 7).

This is the intimate bond for which we were formed. We hunger for significance—to be seen and understood and loved, to be and live *marvelous*—because we are made not only to know God but also to be known by Him. David celebrates this truth when he writes,

> O LORD, You have searched me and known me.
> You know my sitting down and my rising up;
> You understand my thought afar off.
> You comprehend my path and my lying down,
> And are acquainted with all my ways.
>
> —VERSES 1–3

Even as we are known, we are nonetheless born into hiding. "God saw us when we could not be seen," writes Charles Spurgeon, "and he wrote about us when there was nothing of us to write about."[2] For the nine months we are encased in the womb, unseen even by the eyes of the woman whose body labors to give us life, we grow from the size of a seed to that of a watermelon. Unseen, we grow about 1,600 times larger than the tiny union of cells we started out as. In that secret place, we are incubated. Hand-hidden. Known. Witnessed. Concealed. Within the hiddenness of the womb, God gives us a glimpse of a forever truth, the truth that quickens and multiplies in secret.

The problem is not that we long for significance but that

we are shifty or misguided in where we look for it. When we crave most the eyes of others—their opinions and accolades—we break our gaze with the only eyes that will ever truly see us. We forget the beauty of the Creator-eyes turned toward us, the ones that saw the inception of our lives and loved what He saw.

We're *still* hungry for the thing for which we were made: to be seen, to be known, to be celebrated, to participate in something much larger than ourselves. But too often we settle for lesser things. It seems easier to get a like online than it does to get quiet before God, to seek His face and listen for His whispers. Especially if we're not sure what the expression on His face might be or whether His whispers will be kind. We wonder if God could ever like what He sees in us when no one is looking. And we forget it was in that same hiddenness that our selves took shape in the first place.

"He said He loves me, Mommy," my daughter told me as I tucked her in, her words whispered with her hand to her mouth and cupped around my ear. Apparently, it was a secret.

This was years after that summer in the Adirondacks, years after I'd paced the floors of that Barracks Road boutique, and several years into married life. Nate and I had four of our now six children at the time. Those four were adopted—Eden and Caleb from Ethiopia, and Lily and Hope from Uganda. Our children are shedding orphan skin, a process that isn't much different for the rest of us believers in Jesus, shedding their old selves to become who they truly are. We sometimes see our home as a laboratory of the human heart as we witness the transformation of orphaned spirits into true sons and daughters in family room afternoons and over dinner dishes and during soccer practice.

Adoption has a stigma, at times, of broken children being brought into intact environments. While that's partially true, the greater truth is that every one of us is fractured. And even after we find our way into God's arms, parts of us are still broken, still in need of the tender hand of a Father gently putting us back together. Whether twenty-three, forty-eight, or seventy-one, there are always newly vulnerable parts of ourselves that need the reassurance of this wild love of God.

The four hurting hearts in our house truly aren't much different from our own hearts, just less able to mask the pain. They desperately crave a carefree welcome into their daddy's lap and yet are terrified of such boundless love. They often find it easier to dutifully serve and be vigilantly careful never to make a mistake or always to prove their value and their worthiness for love. Their brokenness has taught them to scramble for security in how they perform rather than to find it with a sigh of relief in the stability of their daddy's arms.

As adults, we often accept the language of being a daughter or a son of God and yet still struggle—nearly daily and sometimes hourly—with the internal strife of not knowing how to rest in the safety of our God's arms. We live with Him, under His watch and in His family, and yet still behave like orphans—distant, fragmented, and serving tirelessly to earn our keep.

The Father's pursuit of us doesn't end at salvation. He is forever alluring us. Yet we often live as if we are more comfortable remaining fractured because that's all we know: serving well, and shaming ourselves back to good behavior when we don't. Author A. W. Tozer describes God's relentless faithfulness this way: "Psuedo-faith always arranges a way out to serve in case God fails it. Real faith knows only one way and gladly allows itself to be stripped of any second way or makeshift substitutes. For true faith, it is either God or total collapse. And not since Adam stood up on the earth has God failed a single man or woman who trusted him."[3]

At one time, this was all I'd known of how to relate to Him. But now I get to witness in my children the same healing work that is ongoing within me, the same healing work that I suspect is ongoing in you.

On this particular night, Hope couldn't yet give voice to what she was experiencing, but it was this: *she* was God's secret. This child had known horror in her early childhood. She had taken her first steps on the streets and without a home, dust under her fingernails. No soapy bubble baths in Mommy's bathtub for this wee thing. She couldn't count to ten, but she'd already climbed the mountain of fatherlessness on earth.

Yet God's gaze on her never wavered. She wasn't relegated to second-class status in His eyes when her traumatic early childhood left her developmentally "behind" the typical child. In a culture where babies are learning to read and toddlers are groomed for Harvard, Hope was being kept. By God. And she was starting to know it. She was breaking free from the lie that many of us believe: performance earns our keep.

Her brushes with God—and her awareness of His gaze on her—are my daughter's invitation out of an orphan spirit. They are her mile markers, more firmly charting her course than any SAT score or college acceptance letter or job promotion.

To understand that a Father with kind eyes *sees* us, even in secret, makes daughters and sons out of all of us who struggle to know what it means to call God Daddy. It makes hearts beat again. It turns prayer into intimate whispers between us and the one who made us.

"He said He loves me, Mommy," she told me. And I remembered her first dance recital, not long after she had come home to us. She had practiced her routine in and out of class for a semester. Every one of us in our family knew the steps. She'd spent weeks pirouetting through our kitchen with a dishcloth in hand, performing with confidence on our living room hearth.

But the night of the performance, I could feel her hand shaking in mine as I walked her down the hall to her lineup. I hurried back to my seat in the auditorium as she waited for her group to be called. I was nervous for her. I so wanted this night to be a win.

When she *relevéd* out on stage among twelve other girls, I, like all the other parents, narrowed my eyes onto just my child. But several beats into the routine, I widened my scope and realized she was a step or two behind. Then three. Then four.

The other children moved in synchronized motion while my beautiful girl carefully performed her routine, too focused on her steps to notice how far behind she was. Too inexperienced to skip steps to catch up.

For seven minutes, I looked beyond her slippered feet—out of sync, arms moving in one direction while her classmates' moved in another—and fixed my mind on her story. Alongside the others, my daughter may have been out of step, but she was also stunning. Light and joy cascaded out of her with every twirl. She had come through the fire of loss and death and hardened dreams, and tonight she was *dancing*.

From my seat, I could see her counting steps, her expression serious and focused. But her eyes were alert and glistening under the stage lights, not dull and weighted as they were when we'd first met her at the orphanage months before. She wasn't posing as someone she'd learned to mimic—a common orphan survival skill. She wasn't dancing to impress others. If she had stopped to notice others, she probably would have frozen in panic. Instead, she was costumed in God. He was making a dancer out of a street kid. This was a child who was learning to be loved.

"He said He loves me" weren't words Hope had learned in a Sunday school song. They'd jumped directly from the pages of God's Word into her heart, and they came alive in her dance steps. This was His real love, welling up within her.

After the recital, her daddy and brother showered her with flowers and she chattered away the entire car ride home. She was the belle of the ball. This child who'd grown up a street-smart survivor and who had been called mischievous by orphanage workers became a glowing ballerina that night.

Her costume is now tucked away in a bin labeled with her name. She pulls it out sometimes, as if she can access that night all over again through the chiffon in her fingers.

I didn't show her the recording afterward, because it might tell a different story than the one I saw and the one she lived. Our human eyes can betray the truth of the story we're living. Even I, her mother, didn't see the whole of her that night. The God who formed her is the only one who saw it all.

To her teacher, my tiny dancer was out of step. To the parent sitting one row in front of me, she was one of two dark-skinned girls on stage. To the girl dancing next to her—being primed for a future in ballet—she wasn't good enough yet to be competition. To her mama, she was being restored. To her daddy, she was a doe-eyed princess.

To the one who made her, she was even more.

She was art.

She was fire and wonder.

Marvelous and worth His blood spilled.

She was His story.

She was His to hide. To keep.

And to tell.

My little girl lives in a world that might label her one way, but she is beginning to tune her ear to the one who tells her who *He* sees, who she truly is. She is destined for greatness, this child of mine. Destined to revel in the truth that she is seen even when no one else is looking. Destined to know the voice of the one who talks to her in the dark, even when no one else is listening.

∞

My children aren't the only ones who are surprised by uncon-ditional love. When I struggle to believe I'm loved, I find myself looking for ways to achieve more. (All of this is mostly subconscious.) If unfettered, I have a drive in me to earn love by being a star. When I'm not feeling deeply and uncondi-tionally loved, I try to keep others applauding, because I've forgotten how to listen for Jesus' sweet whispers in my ear.

Just like sweetly feverish Martha.

The night Mary poured perfume on Jesus' feet, her brother, Lazarus, was reclining at table with Jesus, and her sister, Martha, was serving. On a previous evening when Jesus was dining in Bethany, Mary had wasted not perfume but herself at His feet. She wasted time by wasting an opportunity to serve.

In contrast, Martha, the consummate hostess, "was dis-tracted with much serving" (Luke 10:40). Martha scurried to serve, to show her love—and likely to prove her worth—by meeting the perceived needs of her guests. No doubt she was overwhelmed. But she was also distracted from what truly mattered.

"Lord, do You not care that my sister has left me to serve alone?" protested Martha. "Tell her to help me."

But Jesus wasn't irritated with Mary, nor did He consider her lazy. To Him, Mary's choice was an act of radical love. "Martha, Martha, you are worried and troubled about many things," Jesus said. "But one thing is needed, and Mary has chosen that good part, which will not be taken away from her" (vv. 41–42). Mary was so confident in God's love for her that she sat at His feet and listened.

She wasted herself on Him.

So often in our scurry to serve, we forget our starting place, the one thing that is needed.

I had yet to learn this the summer I waited tables at that camp in the Adirondacks. My biggest crisis that summer was not having packed the right clothes to work in a stifling hot dining hall. So I called my mom from the pay phone in the center of the camp and asked her to send me new tank tops. What I didn't say directly but tried to imply was this: *don't send just any tank tops, but please, Mom, cute ones.* My one-month stint of serving behind the scenes gave me an invitation to flirt with tables full of cute boys from all across the country, and I was a bit dual-minded. Perhaps more obvious then was the struggle I still have: I wanted to serve, but I also wanted to be noticed.

But there was one small group on our crew of volunteers who didn't even have the option to be noticed. They were assigned to the affectionately (and appropriately) named area we called "the pits." This crew of six washed dishes in the back corner of the kitchen from just after breakfast until just before they crawled into bed at night. They didn't venture into the dining hall or flirt with campers. And theirs wasn't a rotating assignment—working the pits was their job for the entire month. Many of them had packed cute clothes and comfortable but trendy shoes in preparation for waiting tables. But now when they called home from the pay phone in the center of camp, they were asking their moms to send T-shirts and jeans that could get ruined. There was no time for stain-spotting in the pits' washing line.

I breathed relief when I was assigned to the dining hall. I felt pity for the people in the pits. For an entire month, hardly anyone knew they were there, except for the one night each week when the campers were introduced to our entire work crew. On that one night, our pits crew sat on stage among the one hundred high school and college-aged volunteers and merely stated their name and their job: "I'm Abby from Cincinnati, Ohio, and I work in the pits." In an entire month, they were seen just four times. The other forty-three thousand minutes of their thirty days went unobserved by all but one.

That crew of six fascinated me. I didn't understand the joy that erupted from them many times behind the swinging doors of the kitchen. How could one month in that job truly be fulfilling when they worked unseen? At the time, I didn't know about their early morning Bible studies or the conversations they had with God and each other. I didn't read their journals or see how their hearts for God grew during this month when their clothes dripped with well water and they reeked all day of dish soap and stale breakfast sausage. I just pitied them. And yet something tells me they had an experience that the rest of us in cute tank tops didn't.

I'd be naive to think those sixteen- and seventeen- and eighteen-year-olds on the pits crew loved the hidden corner of the kitchen when they started. Like me, they probably requested an assignment in the dining hall. Maybe they even muttered under their breaths during those first few days—or weeks—of elbows in suds, hearing laughter from the other side of the door where the cute boys and girls crushed on their waitstaff. But likely, they were indoctrinated early into wrestling with hiddenness and how to find Him and thrive there. They had thirty days of focused practice.

Hidden servanthood is drudgery when we're intent on praise from others. And it is also drudgery when we tell ourselves that our desires for recognition and praise don't matter.

How we respond when we are hidden by God is everything.

When we know we are seen by the one who created praise itself and He is the one who gives us a word of affirmation—when He is the one who notices us pouring ourselves out in secret—we realize that this is what we craved all along. We hear His applause. We are celebrated. And something inside of us comes alive. In that one moment, the underground hidden life looks and feels very different.

The pits—whatever they may be for us in any given moment—are no longer awful. Being elbow-deep in soapsuds and breakfast-sausage grease looks and feels different when we know God sees us there.

───────── *For Your Continued Pursuit* ─────────

Genesis 1:26 | Job 28:24 | Job 34:21 | Psalm 90:4 | Psalm 119:32 | Psalm 139 | Psalm 147:5 | Proverbs 15:3 | Ecclesiastes 11:5 | Isaiah 46:9–10 | Matthew 10:30 | Matthew 20:6–7 | Matthew 23:11–12 | Mark 1:35 | Mark 10:45 | Luke 6:12 | Luke 10:38–42 | Luke 22:41–44 | John 12:2–3 | John 17:22 | John 17:26 | Galatians 4:1–7 | Philippians 1:6 | Hebrews 5:7 | Revelation 1:14

three

OPEN HANDS

Living a Story We Had Not Planned

"A woman came having an alabaster
flask of very costly oil."
—MARK 14:3

It was long before morning when I woke up in a cold sweat.
I felt as though I'd been chased in my dreams, except there
was no villain and I wasn't a victim. My pounding heart was
loud against the silence in the house.

The venue of my dream was a ten-year-old girl's birthday
party. My daughter Lily had been invited at the last minute,
and she responded with the youthful thrill that any birthday
invitation incites. But just before she left, we learned that the
event wasn't merely a birthday party; it was a slumber party,
the stuff dreams are made of for preadolescent girls.

True to our waking selves, the dream versions of me and
Nate, knowing Lily's makeup, decided not to let her stay the
night. Most of her childhood had been one big overnight as
she shared sleeping quarters with classmates and friends at
the orphanage. She was still so new to our family that nights

at home within the consistency of her bedtime routine and her father's arms as he tucked her in were necessary for her healing. In the dream, she was crushed by our decision. We spent the rest of the dream explaining to her why we wouldn't let her sleep over. Then I woke up, shivering and too agitated to go back to sleep.

Lying in bed and prayerful, I realized the dream was really about me. As I dreamed it, I'd felt all that Lily might feel. The rush of excitement, then the disappointment. The feeling of being the only one left out. The sting of your parents' betraying you, begrudging you something you want so much.

We were a family of seven by that time, and I treasured each of my children. At times, though, I caught myself feeling empty and dissatisfied. Those were the times I'd look more carefully at the bulletin board in our kitchen where we tack up Christmas cards and leave them up all year. The board was filled with photos of cousins and friends and neighbors, all with combed and styled hair and carefully picked and pressed clothes. Each family looked like what I had once thought my family would look like at this point in my life: Husband with his arm around his wife, children spaced two years apart, all with matching smiles, all secure and happy with albums of baby pictures at home. This was the Christmas card I envisioned when I was twenty-four and newly married. Back when I had a white-knuckled grip on my plans.

I was still pondering the significance of the dream a few days later when I woke one morning and noticed the early streaks of sunrise had just begun to show themselves beyond the woods lining our front yard. They highlighted the encroaching harshness of winter on a landscape that had been lush a few months earlier. Every tree looked dead.

Long dead.

Had I not lived here the winter before, had I not witnessed the routine seasonal transformations, I'd have assumed those trees had no life left in them. All I could see was what was *not* there.

But I knew the trees were not dead. They were merely dormant. In winter, the roots are quiescent. In winter, what we can see with our eyes is not the whole story. Winter gives birth to spring not just in the tree but in us.

At twenty-two and fresh out of college, I knew nothing about winter. I imagined my spiritual life as a tall and opulent tree, each year reaching new heights and bearing dazzling fruit as I grew toward mastery of my relationship with God. I lived to expect and exploit spring and summer—flourishing external growth—but autumn and winter soon followed.

There was frost when my fledgling marriage was chilled by anger and silence, followed by my father's death and—my longest, coldest winter—twelve years of infertility. I was no longer living in a hothouse, always growing taller, always producing fruit. God was winterizing me. His intention wasn't to leave me fruitless—God loves fruit. He hid me so that I would find Him in the hiddenness. So I would come back to my roots, so I would see His eyes on me in the hiding.

When what I see with my eyes doesn't come together like I hope, I tend to look a little bit longer at Him. When my dreams aren't being fulfilled, I'm invited to search the one who gives dreams in the first place. When I'm unproductive or when my greatest feats of productivity leave me empty, I grow hungrier for something more than what I can accomplish with my own hands and drive.

God hides me to show me His kind eyes toward me—gentler than the taskmaster I am toward myself. And He hides me to tell me my story—to remind me of Himself, the author. It is the greatest story my skin will ever know—God, in me, radiating through me, making glory for Him on the earth.

I have a version of my story, a shiny version fit to put on a Christmas card. But God's version is far richer. It's deeper and it's layered with purpose. His version of my story stretches beyond what I can see. It includes more twists and turns, goodness and glory, than my mind can construct.

Yes, I had plans as a college student and a new wife and an adoptive mother of four ready to build an ever-happy family. I have plans today, spoken and unspoken, that I want desperately for God to shape. But my plans often need dormancy. They need a winter—sometimes many winters—to rest. I need time to get caught up in God's seeing me in my unseen moments. Time so that when He breathes the warmth of new plans into me, I actually want them. And so I want Him more than I want the plans themselves.

Most of the time, we don't reach for God until we have to. Our hardest circumstances are often the ones God uses to call forth the deeper reach for Him.

Until I was in over my head with five children, I never needed to pray the Bible under my breath, up the stairs and down, from one bedroom to the next.

Until I sat feeling invisible in a crowd of peers, I never needed to ask God, daily, for strength to be unnoticed.

Until my friends' bellies were round and I was barren and felt forgotten by God, I never prayed the Psalms as if they were my own cries.

Until I was mothering four former orphans and wondering just how far God goes to restore a life, I never scoured the Word of God for truths about restoration.

Until the voices of accolades around me suddenly got quiet, I never saw a need to sit before God in the silence and wait for His whispers.

Until all the other words around me fell short, I never considered meditating upon God's Word, mulling it over and letting it dance around my mind for longer than a morning quiet time.

In all these experiences, it was as if God were the parent in my dream, the one slowly shaping my life from orphan to daughter. *You don't see it all like I do. I know what's best—I know you best. The story you want, though not bad, isn't the story I have for you. Will you let Me write your story?* This is the invitation God offers in the winters of my soul. An invitation to trust that my story is His story. And if I let Him winterize me, He will deepen my roots and help me to stretch my branches toward Him—for my good and for His glory.

Mary of Bethany also had plans, we might suppose. And planners don't like to leave things to chance. Mary carried her plan in a jar around her neck. She held dignity and extravagance near her chest. This spikenard oil was imported from India and cost a year's wages. This was no impulse purchase. It was her assurance—her savings account and her security. She'd likely had it long before she met Jesus, and so it was a part of her. Her scent mingled with the scent of this oil. It marked her. Until she saw a different function for its extravagance.

Yes, it was an extravagance that she carried, but it paled in light of the extravagance she experienced when she was with Jesus.

This man had comforted her when she grieved the death of her brother, had taught her truth and treated her with dignity in a culture that neither educated nor honored women. His kindness and His defiance of cultural norms emboldened her and prepared her to pour out brazen love as oil.

In a moment, her plans suddenly meant nothing to her. Letting go of them, while uncomfortable and unfamiliar, empowered her.

She'd grown safe within this otherworldly love He offered her, so an exchange of her story for His no longer frightened her. She moved from fear to desire. She wanted it more than anything else.

Even the oil.

Mary was so in love with the God who had seen her when no one else did, the God who knew her and whispered His secrets to her, the God who breathed fresh life into her dead brother, that she'd do anything for Him. She would crack open what had once been her treasure in exchange for a new story. It was a costly exchange, but it was worth it because she was His.

I cried when I found them, these two baby teeth carefully wrapped in a foam container, deep in my purse. They'd been there for months.

It had been a particularly hard set of months for my almost-teenager, who was now too old to lose baby teeth. And because it was hard for her, it was hard for all of us. Her struggles had become ours. She was once a photograph on our refrigerator for which we wistfully prayed, and now she was ours to hold and to help heal.

When we said yes to adoption, I said yes to a process and a person I couldn't yet hold or help heal and didn't know. I didn't realize we were also saying yes to mountains of paperwork, paperwork that documented every corner of our lives and invited social workers to comment on it all. The paperwork itself was mostly an inconvenience to my heart—all the systems we had to navigate and all the hoops we had to jump through made my entrance into motherhood feel like a mind-numbing bureaucratic procedure.

But when these heart-imagined children became names and toothy grins on our refrigerator, I started seeing past the paperwork. I also acquired a new ability to live stretched across two continents. When it was 3:00 a.m. in the Midwest, my children were just waking up across the ocean. *What are they doing? Who is shepherding their days? Do they think about us?* I routinely lived and loved and thought in two time zones—starkly and inconveniently parted from my very own children.

As the adoption process continued, I focused only on the

best possible outcomes. I closed my ears to stories of former orphans and their families who thought their biggest battles were the bureaucratic ones, only to discover later the real battles were just beginning when they brought their children home. I was naive when we said yes to adopting older children and outside of the birth order (older than our oldest child). I was convinced we would be different. Our fantastic family chemistry and love would wash over any lasting consequences from their years of loss.

But then that paperwork grew skin, and the stories had faces, and they weren't on the other side of the ocean—they were down the hall.

This particular child whose baby teeth wound up in my purse had lived many undocumented years before she came home to us. We didn't know when she'd lost her first tooth or taken her first step, and those were minor details compared with the pages we'd leave blank on the forms of doctors' offices requesting family history. Getting the twenty-seventh piece of adoption paperwork notarized was nothing compared with all that had gone undocumented in her life, everything from her first word and first step to family records of deaths and births.

By the time she came to us, she rarely wanted to be held. She'd long ago learned to push tears deep into her pillow. Years into having her in our home, loss still hovered over her. All her ouchies were on the inside, not ones a mama could kiss and make better.

So Nate and I spent a focused month praying mostly for her. All the children had their unique needs, but as is often the case in a big family with a lot of noise, you attend to the bell that rings the loudest. Though she'd been home for several years, different circumstances and life mile-markers triggered memories of her painful history. And often at unexpected times. Pain, through the body and life of a child, isn't always tidy. A simple correction could send one of our children spinning for days. An altercation with a sibling might trigger a child to retreat in silent anguish until she could be coerced into talking about the storm inside of her. Adoption amplifies the already-sown mystery of raising tiny, uniquely created human beings. Nate and I found that the first, best tending to the hearts of our children was done in secret with God. So we prayed.

As I watched this child writhe on the inside—in a way that conversation with God gives you an eye to see—I hurt along with her. I felt her loss, but I also felt mine. I grieved for all the life I had missed with my daughter. I grieved for all the times she cried without me there to hold her, without either of us knowing the other's face. I grieved for the story I wanted her to have instead of the one she was living.

I hadn't even been with her when all her baby teeth came out—at least, when most of them came out. A few months before this time of intense prayer, I had taken her to a dentist, who told us that while she had a mouth full of healthy teeth, it was too full. My not so little girl had gained all of her adult teeth while still holding on to two baby teeth. They needed to be removed.

After the extraction surgery (and subsequent rule that this squeamish mama does not witness the early aftermath of surgical procedures), I tucked those two teeth away. Deep enough that I didn't find them until months later, when all the years I'd lost with my daughter were haunting me.

I choked back sobs when I unwrapped that foam box. Oh, the timing!

Our youngest son at the time, the child of my womb, was a baby. He was learning to say Mama and leaving rings of drool on his shirt from cutting his own first teeth. Even as I celebrated his milestones, he was reminding me, day by day, of all I'd never had with my children who were adopted.

I finally admitted that I resented those lost years. I resented them for how they overshadowed my little girl and for the constant worry I felt about whether they always would. I resented that one day she might have a baby of her own and then struggle anew with questions about her birth and childhood I wouldn't be able to answer. I resented that no matter how much love I poured into her, it seemed to always bleed right out again.

There were times I doubled over in pain, haunted by unanswerable questions. *If I resent those lost years, how much more must my child resent them? What kind of pain must she be in? What kind of grief does she feel now that anyone who knew the early days of her life is gone?*

But her baby teeth.

Perhaps He'd been saving them for my finding. Because God was showing me through my child's story that what I'd considered lost was merely hidden.

And hidden—versus lost—changes everything.

There were *always* eyes on her life. Her early years may

not be recorded on pages I can see and hold, but she has a baby book. Every minute of her life has been not only witnessed but recorded. Noticed. Treasured. Loved. My baby, made for an eternal existence with God and held in my arms for the first time when she was seven, had not lost one single day.

I know that my child still needs healing. I know she will need to grieve and walk honestly through her losses. She will need to live into a different story than the one either of us might have chosen for her. And I am committed to be with her in all of it. To grieve with her. And to celebrate those times when she allows herself to be embraced, when we can share tears with one another rather than for one another. So her story is teaching me, her mama who never saw her first baby tooth.

She was made for a life that is witnessed. And though the veil fell thick on her childhood, her childhood wasn't unwitnessed. She was known. My little girl will heal and come to life as she sees herself in God's story.

As will her mama.

——————— *For Your Continued Pursuit* ———————

Psalm 1:3 | Proverbs 3:5 | Isaiah 43:7, 10 | Matthew 6:6 | Matthew 10:29–31 | Luke 10:38–42 | John 11:1–44 | John 15:1–2 | Romans 11:33–36 | 1 Corinthians 2:7–10 | 1 Corinthians 13:12 | Ephesians 3:20–21 | Colossians 1:26–27 | Hebrews 4:13

four

LOVE POURED OUT

Leaning into Our Call to Greatness

"Then she broke the flask and
poured it on His head."
—MARK 14:3

Oh boy, I thought when I heard the conversation from another room. One child was shouting his math facts at the prompting of eager parents. Two plus two didn't require any computation from him. Five plus nine and twenty-three plus seven and sixteen plus three—this child was smart, easily adding numbers when most his age were barely counting fingers.

My children squealed and celebrated, too young to be concerned that another child knew more than they did.

Until one of my daughters chimed in, "Let me play!"

Her age on a transcript would suggest this game would be easy for her too. But I know her history. A simple equation isn't simple for the child who had the slums as her nursery.

"I can count to ten," she announced. "One, two, three, four, seven." She pauses. "Nine, eight . . . ten!"

UNSEEN

All the children in the room cheered, celebrating anything said with a confident gleam.

But I wondered, *How many years does my girl have before she sees her life diminished by another's accomplishments? How many years do I have with her before what she can't do on the outside might wear like shame on her insides?* However, the very next day, my little girl displayed how two storylines can live simultaneously within one person.

It was an entire day full of cousin fun, my children's favorite kind of time. Dress-up clothes and dolls and croquet at Nana's house, in between giggly games of hide-and-seek. Somewhere in the commotion, though, my counting girl had slipped away. She'd holed up in the back office with tape and scissors and markers. She emerged hours later with a stack of love notes. She'd painstakingly made a card for each child, choosing to miss out on a play day she'd been looking forward to for weeks.

She passed out the cards like she was passing out hundred dollar bills, anticipating that each recipient would feel as full in the receiving as she did in the making and the giving. Cousins and siblings threw out a casual thanks for this construction-papered offering, but she didn't seem to notice. She radiated light. She was expressing who she was becoming.

If the sum of our daughter's identity were based on her outward life, Nate and I would be thinking only about her inability to count to ten. *Will she be able to balance a checkbook one day or read* Pride and Prejudice? *Will she study the Bible or give a public speech?*

But there are always two stories in a person—the visible

story and the invisible story—and only one set of eyes that sees them both. David knew the invisible truth: "My frame was not hidden from You, when I was made in secret" (Ps. 139:15).

God has created each of us for greatness. Not the greatness of a stage or a title or a degree, though He may use those things in our lives. He may even let the applause of others encourage us and help us grow. But the sweetest greatness starts with being rooted, being made and nurtured in secret, being seen by God alone.

I graduated from college *magna cum laude*, which is Latin for "with great honor" or "with great praise." I walked across the stage to receive my honors diploma with the pride of one who had turned people toward Jesus during college while still earning good grades. I'd graduated with greatness, or so I thought.

I *craved* greatness.

I vaguely understood that greatness has something to do with internal growth as well as outward accomplishments, but most of what I considered growth could be measured and documented: lives changed, movements started, goals met. If it mattered, I measured it. If I couldn't measure it, it didn't matter.

At the time, I didn't know I could also be great at two o'clock in the morning holding a sick baby or in graciously stepping away from a leadership position at church so someone else could take the limelight. I didn't know that greatness could be had in a years-long journey of fielding the pain of a former orphan or in quietly serving a friend who would never thank me. I didn't know that I might find greatness in leaving my task list unfinished so I could read to a child in my lap. I didn't know at twenty-one with my diploma in hand that I could be great in the dormant seasons—or what I would have then considered unsuccessful seasons. I didn't know that even my very desire for greatness was something that came from God.

Jesus acknowledged this human craving for greatness in the verse I memorized that summer in the Adirondacks: "Whoever would be great among you must be your servant, and whoever would be first among you must be your slave" (Matt. 20:26–27 ESV).

For years, I assumed that this invitation to service—and thereby greatness—was about bringing a meal to a sick friend, volunteering in the nursery at church, or stapling information packets for soccer practice. But the greatness Jesus describes requires more than a slight strain on the pocketbook or the occasional sacrifice of time. He was stating in no uncertain terms that the path to greatness lies in hiddenness. And it's a state of mind and a way of being, not a series of tasks to perform and check off a list.

We become great when we genuinely, happily serve in unacknowledged ways and places because that is where we find the sustaining face of God, especially when no one else sees us or applauds. Hearts that grow in God, that reach for Him and receive His reaching back, become *profoundly* great. Unshakable, even.

At such times, our biggest mistake is to call our hidden-ness accidental. You've probably heard statements like these: "If I could just get out of this transition and into a role where I'm using my gifts . . ." or, "When the kids get a bit older and I can leave the house more . . ." or, "When he's not sick anymore, I'll really be able to give my life away for God's kingdom," or [insert yours here]. We forget that it's in the interruptions, the waiting seasons, the disappointments that we grow best.

It is in those times when we are "sidetracked" by a dis-heartening job, an unshared bed, or a leader who doesn't acknowledge our gifting that God whispers, *This is where you become great—on the inside.*

Mary not only offered God her opportunity for greatness—that jar she carried around her neck—she broke it open. There was no going back. She was all in, and the oil was no longer hers for safekeeping. Mary was now Mary without the oil's musk that had marked her.

In an instant, what had signified security and recogni-tion spilled through her fingers. Those dreams of moving comfortably into old age with financial assurance, and perhaps even thoughts of clothing herself in the finest linens, all fell away as she looked at Him. She was close enough to see the lines on His face. He was beautiful and powerful and safe.

Mary probably hadn't told a soul about this ahead of time. Perhaps she hadn't planned this moment at all. If she had and had told others about it, it's likely they tried to talk her out of it. But they didn't yet know what she knew—that when she got near to Jesus, the glow of everything and everyone else dimmed. When she got near to this man, her life became great. He reveled in her story and in her participation in His story: this was greatness.

There are two stories in a person—the visible story and the invisible story.

To Jesus, Mary's greatness was revealed in the very act that the onlookers called foolish. And in this weakened, wasted greatness, she got closer to Him—she participated in *His* story—and she grew.

Times have shifted. In this digital age, we might well wonder, "If it wasn't posted on social media, did it really happen?" We can't live for the beauty of the hidden life while feeding on likes and comments. As long as we don't make big impact synonymous with greatness, there's nothing wrong with it. But the unintended consequence may be that we think that anything that isn't big and observable isn't great, which renders the rest of life a waiting room. Wasted time. When we live a life of constantly reaching for the next big thing, we miss the greatness God is calling us to right here, right now. In the small, the ordinary, the hidden moments. The white space.

If the chief end of every human being is to glorify God and enjoy Him forever, shouldn't that glory and enjoyment be able to happen when no one is looking? Within the times when we don't seem to be influencing the world at all, the moments when we pour ourselves out at Jesus' feet?

Great kingdom impact comes not just from actions that

make a dramatic and observable impact but from all the accumulated moments we spend looking at God, bringing Him glory in private, and letting Him shape our insides.

We aren't forfeiting outward impact for private devotion to God. We are submitting to the understanding that life in God isn't about God's needing us to do His work for Him or to do it under our own power. It is instead about a glory we can't always measure. It is the work that happens beneath the surface, deep in the soil of our hearts, that in time produces a great harvest of fruit and growth.

Jesus tells us, "But the seed falling on good soil refers to someone who hears the word and understands it. This is the one who produces a crop, yielding a hundred, sixty or thirty times what was sown" (Matt. 13:23 NIV).

Yes, I *am* made to be great. I am made to produce fruit and to bring God glory. So are you. And that desire for greatness can help me start a new nonprofit or invest more in my marriage or adopt a child. Or prompt me to empty out my savings or open a room of my house to someone in need.

But later, when the nonprofit seed cash has evaporated, I'm going to need roots. When the person I've invited into my home leaves in the night and takes my wallet, I'm going to need roots. When the needs of a sick child feel like too much at three in the morning, or the hospital bills exceed my bank balance, I'm going to need roots.

"Some fell on rocky places, where it did not have much soil. It sprang up quickly, because the soil was shallow. But when the sun came up, the plants were scorched, and they withered because they had no root" (vv. 5–6 NIV).

In the context of greatness, we might say that this rocky-place seed accomplished something, at least. But without sinking deep roots into nutrient-dense soil—intimacy with God—it couldn't continue to grow and bear fruit. "But since they have no root, they last only a short time. When trouble or persecution comes because of the word, they quickly fall away" (v. 21 NIV).

Greatness begins underground. In secret. I have to sink my roots deep in the knowledge of God's love to grow branches that bear fruit in and out of season.

No one may notice if you exchange your earbuds and workout music for desperate whispers to God while you pound it out on the treadmill. No one except Him.

And your roots sink deep.

No one may notice if you curl up with your journal and spend time with God on the back porch before sticky-fingered children, just off the school bus, run clamoring through the front door.

But your roots sink deep.

No one may notice if you exchange your smartphone for His Word on your bedside table and check in with Him before checking email every morning.

Here, your roots sink deep.

No one may notice if you pray fiercely and secretly for a friend's ministry to grow, even though you crave the attention she is getting.

Your roots sink deep again.

No one may notice if you turn down a business opportunity in order to spend more quiet hours with God, or if you say no to an opportunity to serve someone in need because you ask Him and He whispers, "I have another plan to meet that need."

Our growing root system reaches and creeps and drinks, deeply, of a greatness that the world can't measure, a greatness that even some within the Christian community might not recognize or understand. But the long-term greatness of a tree is always found in the depth and health of its roots.

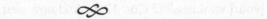

It was one of those 3:00 p.m. meltdowns that had become painfully familiar. I was in the laundry room, pulling wet clothes from the washer and shoving them into the dryer for the third time that day. Clothes that would be worn and discarded and back in the laundry room within the next twenty-four hours.

The laundry itself wasn't daunting; it was just a reminder of all of the other parts of my day that were on a vicious cycle: One child's sunken demeanor as she struggled to speak positive words (again). Another child's terse words and her sister's flashpot response. Another child who still couldn't read.

Then, like ticker tape through my head, in rolled all the things I'd hoped to accomplish that I still hadn't managed to do. I had been full of dreams for this year and had accomplished (maybe) one. I had intended to read a long book with each of the kids individually. I'd finished a chapter each at best. I had plans to teach them to cook and a stack of recipe books we'd not yet cracked open. My pantry was full of ingredients for the Saturday baking days we had never done even once. Weakness crowded into me in that tiny laundry room. No one but Nate knew how trapped I'd felt recently, sandwiched between my children's unrelenting needs and my greater hopes for our family.

Then came the interruption. A phrase, dropped into my mind from Him, softening me as I heard it: *I like you when you're weak.*

It was true. Biblical. "My strength is made perfect in [your] weakness" (2 Cor. 12:9). And now near.

God's power came when I had nothing left. It was perfected there in the cramped laundry room amid loads of wet clothing, loads of unmet needs in my house, loads of unrealized hopes. Loads of unwitnessed hours. Realizing that God saw me and even liked me changed everything about that unseen day.

On days like that, I want His Word more than soundbites I can read online.

On days like that, I crave conversation with God over texting a girlfriend.

On days like that, I see the thrill in searching Him out, knowing He longs to be found. I see spending time with Him—His Spirit breathing through the pages of His Word—as something I desire, not a duty. Verses I've read a dozen times or more become real to me when I have a brush with Him on a hard day.

"Pray without ceasing," writes Paul (1 Thess. 5:17). I want to talk with God throughout my day, even when I'm a mess, because I know He's not looking away from my story but whispering into it.

"Be still, and know that I am God" (Ps. 46:10). When His Spirit blows a light breeze into a stale and difficult day, I want to let it waft over me, refresh me as I sit still before Him.

In conversation with God, my thinking changes. Out of my desire to "be filled with the Spirit," speaking the truth of the Psalms helps me to let go of the vile lies I too often mutter over myself. And I don't have to force myself to do it. I *want* to make a "melody to the Lord with [my] heart" (Eph. 5:19 ESV). On days when I see God seeing me, the notes of a song naturally well up within me.

It's on these days that the places of my life that no one but God sees become the places for the greatest spiritual growth. Just like my baby has growth spurts at unexpected times—his ankles shoot right out from his pant legs—I find my love for God often grows most without noise or fanfare.

When our eyes are locked on our outward lives, we inevitably assess our growth by the "success" of our circumstances. But the heart can grow at any time. And God is all eyes for heart growth. "The LORD does not look at the things people look at. People look at the outward appearance, but the LORD looks at the heart" (1 Sam. 16:7 NIV).

Four more loads of laundry to do and evening is encroaching. Your underground heart in God can grow right here.

A presentation for work goes sour. Your internal life in God can grow, minutes after it's over.

Third date with a guy you've started to like and you realize that he wants this one to be the last. This is where your insides can reach for God and grow.

The dream of writing a book, shelved alongside your

rejected manuscript, another closed door. This may be your greatest chance to grow, when no one sees and no one applauds.

Or maybe you've achieved your big goal or gotten the big promotion but still go home from the celebration party feeling empty, anxious that you won't be able to do what others expect. Even in your greatest successes, you get to have secret conversations with God. He sees you offstage and on Saturdays, away from your position.

Our growth in Him can happen at any venue and in any season of life. Whether or not our tasks, our careers, our families seem to be successful at the time. And the times that God hides us, sometimes away from success or applauding hands, are often the times when our roots reach deeper into the earth. We grow, down.

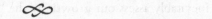

"She could go far with this," my daughter's piano teacher told me. "She picks it up quickly. She's advancing fast."

Whether in piano or sewing or art or math, my Renaissance girl is a quick study. Nate and I put her in a unique class that taught both music skills and praying God's Word because we wanted to see a tuning in her heart. We wanted to stretch her ability to play the piano alongside her reach for God.

The other children in class were a head shorter than her and years younger, yet my daughter felt intimidated. She'd grown up among bullies scavenging for any piece of security

LOVE POURED OUT

the orphanage could afford them, often at the expense of the
quiet ones like her.

Two weeks into the class, she was invited to play while
others sang and prayed. She'd mastered her latest piece in
one week at home, pouring herself out over the keys while I
was across the hall in my office and her siblings were upstairs
building Lego villages. She'd often walk past the piano on her
way up the stairs, only to find herself pulled back to the chair
to play for just a few more minutes.

This was all when she thought no one was watching.

So it was in a rush of uncharacteristic bravery that she
agreed to play for a dozen sets of eyes. But when the moment
came, those eyes became like the ones haunting her memory.
That midwestern classroom became a dirt courtyard in Africa.
She convinced herself that she saw the teachers roll their eyes
at each other while she played.

My skilled piano player missed nearly every chord,
according to her teary description when she got home. A
teacher kindly rushed to her rescue, coaching her with basic
piano instructions but causing her little heart to sink even
farther into shame. *Maybe I really do stink at this*, she thought.

The class shifted and another child, three years younger,
took the bench and played seamlessly.

She ran into my bedroom as soon as she came home. "It
was awful," she said. "I'm so embarrassed." She told me how
her fingers fumbled and a younger child got the applause.
"Now everyone thinks I'm a terrible piano player," she
moaned.

If she had played in public the way she does in private, the room would have swelled with applause. The other students would look at her differently when she came for class next time. They'd see her no longer as the shy child in the back but as the girl with great promise on the keys.

But God had another plan for that Friday afternoon. He was forging her in hiddenness, offering her a private invitation to sink her roots in Him and grow.

So my beautiful girl and I pressed pause on the ruckus in her head, the perceptions of others and the embarrassment and imaginary jeers. We asked God what He thought about that moment.

She quieted the internal noise and heard a whisper.

"I think He liked that I got up there to play," she said with the first smile I'd seen from her since the class.

What her human audience might have thought and what her wounded imagination perceived were both drastically different from what God thought of her. At the tender time of youth, she knew that God liked what He saw in her—yes, even her weakness. And she grew that day as both a pianist and a child of God. God had a message for my girl that afternoon that sank deeper into her soul than a round of applause. He used her weakness, the weakness she resented, to hide her. He spoke a whisper she could hear only if she leaned, just a little more, into Him.

Hidden behind fumbling fingers, she asked Him the question she might never have asked if she had wowed the crowd with her keyboard skills: *What does God think about that moment? What does He think about me?*

God shielded her from her own idea of greatness and invited her to know His thoughts of her instead.

Her roots grew deeper that day. And it was the beginning of true greatness.

──────── *For Your Continued Pursuit* ────────

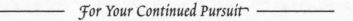

1 Samuel 16:7 | Psalm 1:3 | Psalm 37:4 | Psalm 46:10 | Psalm 52:8–9 | Jeremiah 17:7–8 | Matthew 5:19 | Matthew 13:5–6 | Matthew 13:21–23 | Matthew 18:4 | Matthew 20:26–27 | John 15:1–8 | Romans 8:18–19, 24–25 | 2 Corinthians 12:9 | Ephesians 3:17–21 | Ephesians 5:19 | Colossians 2:6–7 | 1 Thessalonians 5:17

five

UNCOVERED

Becoming Vulnerable

> "She wiped His feet with her hair."
> —JOHN 12:3

I didn't realize we were going to a house party, I thought, feeling uncomfortable even before I crossed the threshold of this home we were visiting just a few years after being married. The walls of the brownstone reverberated with song, and heat from dozens of warm bodies packed inside made the windows sweat against the winter air.

A local worship band was belting out a familiar praise song, and the living room furniture had been moved to accommodate sound equipment and standing guests. This was a homemade mashup of rock concert and church—a party among friends, except we knew only the couple who'd brought us. Nate and I glanced at each other, exchanging a wordless question: *You sure we should stay?*

That's when I saw her.

Eyes closed, arms raised, body swaying. She looked to be in her fifties or sixties, lost in a dance that reminded me of what I'd picture to be a 1960s rock concert. She was all "out there," seemingly with no awareness that she might be making a spectacle of herself. First, I judged her. Then I speculated. *Who is her audience? Who exactly is she doing this for?*

I was familiar enough with my unfortunate habit of rushing to judgment to know that I needed to pause from these thoughts. So I decided to pray for this woman in an effort to win over my critical thoughts. As quickly as the judgment entered my mind, another thought followed: *You don't know what she's been through.*

My prayer continued intermittently throughout the evening. For some reason, I couldn't take my eyes off this woman. Because my default mode was judgment, I'd recently begun to practice asking God to show me His heart for people. As I prayed for God's heart for her, one thought came: *She's like Mary.* It came to me as my own thought, but I suspected it was a whisper from God. After all, the woman who poured out her alabaster livelihood to anoint Jesus was one of my favorites, and this woman at the party—well, I wasn't seeing her actions in a favorable light.

But then I felt a divine nudge to tell this woman what I was thinking—that she reminded me of Mary. *Ugh. I don't want to do that,* I thought. *Wouldn't talking to her only validate her attention-seeking behavior?* (Another one of judgment's lies: that I was somehow responsible for correcting this woman's behavior.)

Even so, I hesitantly approached her at the back of the room where she now stood.

"I've felt a nudge to pray for you tonight," I said somewhat awkwardly, shouting above the worship band and not exactly looking her in the eye. "As I prayed, I saw you to be like Mary of Bethany."

She looked away, and then back at me. "You don't know what I've been through," she said.

I was speechless.

"In the past seventeen months, I've lost both my son and my husband," she said. "They both died. Worshiping God is the only place I find joy."

I was silenced, reminded again how getting even an inch deep into someone else's unseen story can change everything. Maybe I'd come to the party just for this, just for her.

In the decade that followed—the first decade of our marriage—I got to be this woman. Not because I learned to dance so freely in front of others but because I had my own story of loss and emptiness. I had a barren womb with little hope for healing, and reaching for God became the only way I could find joy. I canceled Friday night plans so I could stay home and pray. I rearranged my schedule so I had more time to cry and lament over my Bible. I propped up His Word on the treadmill at the gym, determined to use every available moment to soak in every line I could. I was falling in love with God through pain, caring less and less what others thought of me. Like the woman at the party, my response to my losses made me a little weird too. I was grieving and bleeding and needed a new sort of encounter with the God who is near to the vulnerable and brokenhearted.

Barrenness is about what you don't have, so it often goes undetected. I was sick—my body wasn't working—but I didn't have crutches or a sling. I had only my unchanging waistline. Like the grieving woman at the party, I had a story no one knew unless they took the time to ask. And few asked. My untold story forced me into a season of vulnerability before God, all while He hid me from the eyes of others.

The "Mary" I met at the party that night poured herself out at Jesus' feet not out of duty but because He was all she had left. Her circumstances had stripped her of everything but one truth: *He is all I have, He is husband to me, and His love is stunning.* She gave Him the kind of worship one can give only from a thin place—a place where the separation between this world and eternity seems to dissolve, a place where we believe and experience God's love in a visceral way.

My empty womb ushered me into that thin place, the place where I began to believe—not just say—that God's love is real. With every bleeding day, I was forced to reveal myself, in pain, before His eyes. And that's when I discovered how truly beautiful His eyes are. Only then could I pour myself out at His feet with unhinged, unembarrassed, extravagant devotion.

In Mary's day, hair was a woman's glory and her covering. Jewish women uncoiled their hair only for private moments within their own homes. To let down one's hair in public was scandalous behavior—and exactly what Mary did that night as Jesus reclined at the table. She not only let down her hair but also "took a pound of very costly oil of spikenard, anointed the feet of Jesus, and wiped His feet with her hair" (John 12:3).

Mary wiped Jesus' feet with her *hair*. She unwound the covering she'd hidden behind, her adornment, and used it to anoint Jesus' dirty feet. Her earthly glory brushed up against the Savior's humanity. Improper. Disgraceful. She used her covering and glory as a rag.

The men around the table judged her.

But the Son of God was moved.

Hers was an extravagant devotion. Adoration with God alone in mind. She chose to be vulnerable before the one who already knew her deepest longings. And Jesus called her vulnerability beautiful.

Mary did what few of us will allow ourselves to do: she disregarded both the approval and disapproval of those around the table so she could give the most outwardly beautiful part of herself to Jesus. Right in front them. Unashamed at her lack of restraint. She allowed herself to become unhinged in her expression of love. She lived out what she and all of humankind were created to crave: an unhindered, unashamed reach for God.

I was twenty-three. It was on a moonlit September night in Virginia, when the air still felt heavy like summer, that I told Nate I couldn't stop thinking about him. I blurted it out in an uncharacteristic rush of emotion. Our relationship changed in an instant with that admission, though we sat still in the car, letting the words hang as if they were echoing.

We didn't say much as time passed in his car, parked next

to my office, nestled in the windy streets of the old university town where we lived. I shifted and accidentally brushed his knee, and it was a touch as electric as those blurted words had been. I think I fell in love that night.

I'll never again make the turn onto Chancellor Street without remembering it as the place where everything changed. Where I surrendered to the vulnerability of love.

I have similar feelings about the dozens of places where I've surrendered to the vulnerability of love with God. Tender times when He cupped His hands around my story and hid me. My words to Him were raw, unfiltered, awkward. But He was tender and responsive. These were the ripest conditions for love to grow. When I was uncharacteristically vulnerable, He hid me in His love and drew me near.

Those vulnerable experiences with God have a way of sticking with us just like Chancellor Street does in my story with Nate. "In the secret place of His tabernacle He shall hide me," writes the psalmist (Ps. 27:5). Yet we still tend to avoid that kind of vulnerability with God. Our experiences of vulnerability with other flawed human beings too often leave us guarded and cautious. We shrink back from baring our souls. It's not safe. So we partake in the most elusive form of hiding: we hide from God.

We aren't the first.

Then the eyes of both of them were opened, and they knew that they were naked; and they sewed fig leaves together and made themselves coverings.

And they heard the sound of the LORD God walking

in the garden in the cool of the day, and Adam and his wife hid themselves from the presence of the LORD God among the trees of the garden.

Then the LORD God called to Adam and said to him, "Where are you?"

So he said, "I heard Your voice in the garden, and I was afraid because I was naked; and I hid myself."

—GENESIS 3:7–10

Adam and Eve were the first but certainly not the last to hide from God. Nakedness before God—the creator of blood, bone, sinews, and flesh—became the shared fear of humanity when Adam and Eve sinned. In their shame and embarrassment, they hid.

"Embarrassment is actually sin," says my husband, who knows my self-protective and self-preserving ways. I might say instead, "Embarrassment reveals sin." It might happen like this:

We've had friends over for dinner, and I've fumbled through expressing something near to my heart. I mixed words and misrepresented myself. I'm embarrassed the next morning, regretting that I doled out personal intimacies in a way that wasn't received. My embarrassment reveals that my highest goal is to preserve the image I've given of myself. I lash myself instead of talking to God.

I am afraid because I am naked. And I hide myself from God in self-condemnation.

I'm three minutes down the road from the house that held that baby shower, all those women corralled around one round belly, celebrating, and I want to defame them in my mind. I want to défend myself as a woman who still has value despite not being able to enter their rite of passage. I want to judge them for not recognizing my ache amid their cheers. I'm ashamed of what I don't have, so I criticize those who have it.

I am afraid because I am naked. And I hide myself from God in anger.

There are six small bodies in the car, but it feels like ten. The two in the far back have been bickering, and the babe is hungry and tired. One of my girls is hurting deeply, she stares blankly out the window, lost within her mind. I look behind the seat and discover remnants of last week's lunch molding on the floor mats. *How long until bedtime?* I wonder, eager for this day to be done. I'm resenting my role as a mother today, and even more, my response to it. How can I go to God like this?

I am afraid because I am naked. And I hide myself from God while simply waiting for this hard moment to pass.

These bare places are invitations. God invites us to exchange what feels raw and vulnerable for His strength. God never intended for us to hide from Him, to live with parts of us untouchable to Him. It's in those naked-place moments— the times we allow ourselves to be exposed before God—that He covers us with Himself, blankets us in His safe love, and replaces our exposed weakness with His strength.

"For Adam and his wife the LORD God made tunics of skin, and clothed them" (Gen. 3:21). Even after we've been exposed by our sin and failures, God covers us. He restores what feels like shards from the broken parts of our story and hides us in Himself, all so that we can take the risk to unveil ourselves before Him again.

Who told you that you were naked? asked the God who sees every part of us. And He teaches us the safe place to be seen.

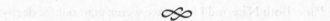

Shortly after we'd adopted Eden and Caleb, a Christian counselor friend who'd worked with children for years observed them playing in his waiting room. We'd described to him their first few months at home with us, and he witnessed what we'd said and more. Even when we weren't within immediate reach, they played freely and without fear. They took delight in trinkets, but even more so in one another, as ones who were already siblings before they became our family. Their eyes were bright with curiosity and playfulness, not deadened or dull.

"There's a word for that," our friend said. "They are 'invulnerables.'"

He spoke to what we'd hoped was true—that Eden and Caleb showed little signs of the loss that had shrouded the years before they could even walk. Despite their traumatic beginnings, the souls of our children—former orphans—had been preserved.

I was relieved.

We'd said yes to them, our first two children to bring home, knowing full well what the experts said about the possible implications of early abandonment. We hung on to optimism more than we did to hope. Optimism is often naive, but hope is forged. (We were too new at this to have forged real hope.) Eden would always stand up for her little brother,

Caleb, and lean into me as Mommy. Caleb would trust. Their eyes would always be bright with expectation. They were the rare kind of "normal" that comes out of abnormality.

Phew. Both Nate and I knew we weren't cut out for deep-seated pain as new parents. So we called them the Invulnerables and exhaled in relief.

Until one day we couldn't anymore.

Growth and time and new siblings added to the mix a few years later revealed worn edges that two-on-two hadn't. One struggled to trust. Another to receive love. The brightness in their eyes waned for a time. A little bit of pressing and we saw tired years behind those wide smiles. Life had worked them over before we held them for the first time. They weren't as invulnerable as they once appeared. But really, is anyone?

I don't relish thinking of myself as vulnerable. I resent the tears I cry over missing my dad when something reminds me of him in the middle of someone else's birthday dinner. I cringe to think I may have "over shared" with a new friend over coffee. I blush when my child says something inappropriate in public. I don't want to send the text for the third day in a row that begs, "I need prayer." I feel naked before the friend with two older (more composed) children who stops by unexpectedly and sees my wreck of a house on a Tuesday afternoon.

Really, who *doesn't* want be an invulnerable? We've bought into the lie that exposing our hearts—in even the smallest of ways—brings only pain. And we take that lie into our exchanges with God.

The one who makes that 9:00 p.m. crisis call to friends

to say, "Our marriage is stuck. Can we come over and get some help?" wakes up to a morning-after "Why didn't we just deal with it ourselves?" gulp of shame. The fifty-year-old single woman who musters courage to whisper to her Bible study group, "I'd like to be married. Would you pray that I might meet someone I could love?" leaves the night feeling foolish for putting herself out there. The wannabe songwriter performs with passion the first song he ever wrote and receives only a smattering of polite applause. He steps off the stage promising himself he will never take a risk like that again. The woman with the baby in the NICU asks God—out loud and in front of the medical staff—to save her son despite his terminal diagnosis, only to wonder, *What if God doesn't come through? What will everyone say about my wild, foolish prayers?*

And yet vulnerability, to God, is beautiful. It incites Him. He moves *in* and near when we are vulnerable. "The LORD is near to those who have a broken heart," writes the psalmist (Ps. 34:18). We all have parts of ourselves that are broken. He invites us to expose those broken parts to Him. As authors Dan Allender and Tremper Longman describe it, "Brokenness is the antidote to shame."[4]

If I allow myself to be vulnerable with God only during the big crisis but not the morning-after embarrassment, whole continents of my heart will remain dark and hidden from the only light that can heal them. And God wants to heal them all. I pray for "more of God," but I rarely grow in personal, intimate understanding of Him without first becoming vulnerable.

To be an invulnerable is to be impenetrable. But those

who turn to God and hide their otherwise-shamed faces in His chest? Those are the ones who hear His heartbeat.

We haven't been hidden by God to suffer or to be punished; we've been wooed into hiding to meet with the God who turns vulnerability into communion. And, yes, this is true not just for our wounds but even in response to our sin. Many times it is our sin that causes us to erect walls and become hardened and distant to God. God draws us into the vulnerability of exposure that comes with repentance. And in the wake of our returning to Him, we find communion. We lean a little bit more into surrender.

God welcomes our most vulnerable selves not simply because He already witnesses every unseen moment of our lives. He welcomes us when we're vulnerable because He knows what it is like to be vulnerable.

Author C. S. Lewis states it this way: "God could, had he pleased, have been incarnate in a man of iron nerves, the Stoic sort who lets no sigh escape him. Of his great humility he chose to be incarnate in a man of delicate sensibilities who wept at the grave of Lazarus and sweated blood in Gethsemane . . . He has faced all that the weakest of us face, has shared not only the strength of our nature but every weakness of it except sin. If he had been incarnate in a man of immense natural courage, that would have been for many of us almost the same as his not being incarnate at all."[5]

Jesus' body broke. He subjected Himself to weakness, though without sin.

Jesus experienced perhaps the most severe form of hiding as He was laid in the "dust of death" (Ps. 22:15). He was naked, disrobed, and mocked by men His hands had formed. Hidden from their understanding. The Son of God who had no sin within Him was vulnerable to the death.

The God whose Spirit enables the breath inside my chest endured a far worse rejection than I ever will. From that vulnerable place, Jesus cried out words through the mouth of David: "Do not be far from Me" (Ps. 22:19). And these are the words He invites us to pray from the depths of our own vulnerability. In His weakness, when He was poured out like water, He gave us permission to be vulnerable, undone. And our vulnerability, only a mere shadow of His, can call up the same cry within us: *God, be near.*

This nearness is most brilliant when I am most weak, here at the nexus of hiddenness and vulnerability before God. He redefines my circumstances even without changing them. When that happens, I no longer resent being hidden, because now I share with Jesus the devastating pain of human rejection. He is no longer just familiar to me. He is the one whose callused, earth-stained fingers gently hold the tender parts of my heart, the raw and bleeding parts of me. He is the one who loves for me to be exposed before Him, leaning in.

Soon after having kids, Nate and I decided that Saturday, not Sunday, would be our day of Sabbath rest. And Saturdays are my weekly reminder of just how much I resist being vulnerable.

We stay in our jammies on Saturdays. We boil the teapot,

several times. Nate and I read our Bibles and books while the kids build forts in the woods and upstairs. We go for walks and let the laundry sit and leave the kitchen a mess—for just a few hours. We breathe, soaking in new ideas and old truths about this God who loves us and hides us close. I read poetry.

It sounds like bliss, but around 2:00 p.m. every Saturday, that same dreaded feeling creeps into my chest. The respite of unplanned hours wears off, and I move into the empty space of the afternoon. I start to wonder, *Who am I with all this time and nothing accomplished with it?*

On Saturdays, I'm reminded of why Sunday through Friday's schedule tempts me to fill it. Too much space and time not filled with boxes to check and tasks to accomplish and worlds to change leave me feeling naked. Exposed. *Who am I without my accomplishments? Who am I without my to-do list?*

As with Adam and Eve in the garden of Eden, our humanity requires coaxing to come out of hiding before God. It is often much easier to obey God's rules than to allow our souls to lean into a fuller surrender of ourselves unto Him. Surrender is vulnerable, and this choice to risk vulnerability with God takes practice. Observing a Sabbath makes this practice frequent. And frequently painful.

I come to those afternoons feeling a combination of empty, squirmy, and uncertain. But He always slides His hand into mine and opens a new world to me—my deeper thoughts, my true feelings, the undercurrent of emotions I've kept buried underneath busy.

I used to say, "Life stops on Saturday in the Hagerty home." This was when I still held on to vestiges of the belief that productivity is the marrow of life. But the empty feeling that persisted on the days when life unproductively "stopped" made me vulnerable and eventually opened a new side of me to God, the side that was safely inviting me to do more than just obey, but to surrender. Now I say, "Saturdays are when life happens in our home." Saturdays are when I am less busy, more weak. Less accomplished, more present. Saturdays are when I fall a little more in love with God. Saturdays are a step toward a deeper surrender.

We have a petri dish of a home. Having eight different bodies doesn't mean only eight different personalities and eight different body types. In our house, we have eight different beginnings, started in three different countries and cultures.

Some people call my toddler son, Bo, or my newborn daughter, Virginia—the ones my body gave birth to—"my own," but all of my children are my own. However, even as I notice each of my children in their uniqueness, I sometimes use Bo as my benchmark to better recognize and understand any differences between how he and his siblings relate to me and reach out for connection.

Several summers ago when I was away from my children for a night, I lay on a hotel room bed and talked to God and had a rush of understanding about my kids—and about beautiful, confident vulnerability.

"Up, please." In my mind's eye, I saw Bo's wide eyes and outstretched arms.

My babe looks up at me with expectation and says this one phrase more times in a day than I can count. It's the first one he learned. At 7:30 a.m., he's squeaking it, his voice rusty from sleep and his body ready to be held. At 9:30 a.m., it's a cry for relief. He's been in the sibling-care rotation and needs the steadiness of Mommy's arms. Sometimes it's said with a quivering lower lip and eyes brimming with tears.

"Up, please"—the incessant plea of the well-tethered child. Up from the world of blocks and puzzles and rowdy siblings and back into the place of sure safety. All day long, I'm reminded that I have one who needs me. One who *knows* he needs me.

Four others need me too. But they never got to say, "Up, please." Instead, they bury their "up, please" behind eyes that don't cry or that cry as a way of trying to manipulate love. Shame and rejection can shove that vulnerable "up, please" way down, as if to say, *I never again want to feel that ache of needing and not receiving, so I won't ask the question that leaves me with my arms in the air and no one on the other side to pick me up.*

"Up, please" is a dangerous request for any of us who question love. Somewhere after saying yes to Jesus, life taught us that "up, please" is for babies. And we don't want to be babies to God.

"Truly I tell you," Jesus said, "unless you change and become like little children, you will never enter the kingdom of heaven" (Matt. 18:3 NIV). This verse is on our grandmother's wall and in cartooned storybooks. We know it by heart. But if we're honest, we don't really like it.

I'd rather not be like a child. I don't want to fumble over my words in a crowd. I don't want my eyes to be red at church from a "discussion" I had with my husband in the car. I don't want to be pushing forty and needing to ask, *What broke at fifteen to make me still keep struggling with that same issue?*

I don't want to be diapered and drool.

To be honest, I don't really want to need God.

Instead, I want to crawl out of weak skin and take notes on a five-point lecture on how to grow my love for God, because wouldn't we all rather learn the hard lessons about love in a tidy sermon than in the rough-and-tumble of our lives? Yet He keeps inviting me to be bare with Him, to sit before Him and let down my heart and ask the questions and wait on His answers. *Be vulnerable and stay vulnerable* is quite the invitation in a world that praises and rewards the invulnerables. The dozen moments in a day that I resent because they remind me that I'm weak are the ones when God wants to hear my faltering voice: "Up, please."

Needy tears have become a treasure in our house. When pain spills out through eight- and ten- and eleven-year-old versions of "up, please," we celebrate. We give long cuddles to reaffirm that raw, vulnerable hearts are hearts on their way to coming alive.

Hey, you in hiding, where are the places you're working hardest to be strong? What causes you to shut down on a given day? What is it that makes you want to send a panicked text to a friend or to escape behind a screen or to rummage in the fridge for something to eat? Where are the places you're coaching yourself to be tough?

Invite God there.

Sometimes we are all too familiar with those places in our lives, but other times it takes practice to recognize them. Search His Word and ask Him to teach you about *you*, and to teach you about Him, right in the midst of the rawest, weakest parts of your life.

Mary let down her hair and elicited a gasp from those around her as she did. Yet with this one act, she inched herself away from self-protection and into the presence of God. Into a deeper surrender to Him. Her moment can be ours, every day. Ask God to help you let down your hair in vulnerability, in adoration. For Him.

My babe cries an "up, please" about as often as I need to say an "up, please" of my own. My vulnerable heart, and your vulnerable heart, needs routinely to climb into God's lap. The more we reach up for God, the more we'll grow, and in the hidden corners of our hearts, the more willing we'll become to choose vulnerability again. To inch toward a deeper surrender to Him and to His story for our lives. When we acknowledge our frailty before God, He offers us wisdom and strength. The psalmist understood this truth when he prayed, "Behold, You desire truth in the inward parts, and in the hidden part You will make me to know wisdom" (Ps. 51:6).

Stop hiding from God. Come out, vulnerable and raw before Him with new strength. *His* strength. Sit at His feet and allow the warmth of His tender eyes to bore through you, to see what's most vulnerable in you, and to respond to it.

──────── *For Your Continued Pursuit* ────────

Genesis 3:7–11 | Genesis 3:21 | Psalm 5:3 | Psalm 7:9 | Psalm 18:6 | Psalm 22 | Psalm 26:8 | Psalm 27:5 | Psalm 31 | Psalm 34:18 | Psalm 51 | Psalm 63:5–7 | Psalm 91:4 | Psalm 119:151 | Psalm 145:18 | Hosea 2:14–15 | Matthew 18:3 | Matthew 27:35–37 | John 1:16 | John 12:3 | John 15:9 | Romans 8:1–2 | Romans 11:17–18 | 1 Corinthians 11:15 | 2 Corinthians 4:7–12 | 2 Corinthians 5:16–20 | 2 Corinthians 12:7–10

INVITATION TO WONDER

Training Our Eyes to See God's Beauty

"And the house was filled with
the fragrance of oil."
—JOHN 12:3

Hope had been working for days on a project that was nondescript and yet time intensive.

She carried her colored pencils in a pouch that she pulled out whenever she had spare minutes. She discreetly slid her work into a basket of books beside her bed when we came to tuck her in at night. She seemed as giddy about the secret creativity as she was about the upcoming reveal.

Finally, the day came when Hope tiptoed into my bedroom with her hands behind her back. It was as if her person was so linked to this project that both the art and her body needed to carry this sacred surprise in a whisper.

"See, Mommy?" she said as she held out a collection of folded pages in front of her. Her face beamed with the sweet confidence of a child who knows she created something beautiful. She'd spent weeks working in anticipation of my delight—she knew I'd love it. And of course I did—in that way that a parent sees focused attention and sweat and persistence as the real prize of any project.

Hope had written a book—a book! My child, still in early readers, had copied drawings from other books and cobbled together phrases to "tell the story of Jesus." The gospel story was intermingled with sketches from *Little House on the Prairie* and *Paddington Bear*—a child's version of how God stretches across all of her scenery.

She wanted to be just like her mommy: a writer. Never mind that she was still sounding out three- and four-letter words, my child wanted to be just like me.

Children often mimic their parents. At five, I wanted to be a teacher, just like my parents. Our son Caleb used to push an overused and ailing baby stroller alongside Nate while he mowed the lawn. Three of our older girls have clanked across our bathroom tiles in my high heels, talking about dates with their husbands and weddings they're attending. At nearly two, Bo made a baby out of a plush pig. He held the pig like I hold him. While I type these pages, eleven-year-old Lily sits beside me with a stack of poetry books and a sketchpad, just like her mommy.

We are, all of us, created to be image bearers. It is written into our DNA.

God made us to wear another's likeness.

His.

"Then God said, 'Let us make man in our image, after our likeness'" (Gen. 1:26 ESV).

So we naturally search within our stories for images to

bear. And then we mimic what we see. Our mimicking begins when we are infants and continues as we age. During the metamorphosis from child to adult, we either begin to see God within our story or we begin to work the room in search of another image to bear. Often it's a little of both.

Daily, these little decisions to look up at God or look around at everyone else might seem insignificant, but only until we get backed into the corner of our circumstances or placed in a season of hiddenness. Then whatever image it is that we've been mimicking reveals itself for what it is—lasting or temporal, truth or facade.

"The lamp of the body is the eye," Jesus says (Matt. 6:22), and my eye can look many directions in one single day without ever leaving home. It's possible for me to see my best friend from first grade winning a mother-daughter footrace and another friend's op-ed in the *New York Times*. I can see my sister traveling to Europe and my cousin's first sale in the business she launched. I can see that an acquaintance from church spent her morning with her Bible and a cup of tea. All in a brief glance at a screen.

Offline, I can see a mother who's ushered her four children under five (all in matching outfits with their hair combed) into a coffee shop, and a neighbor who's come back from a five-mile run. I can see a lawn with fewer weeds than ours and a car with less rust and a home that has a pool. I can see a physically fit mom pushing a stroller effortlessly and another wearing a cute pair of new pumps.

These are all fine things to notice and admire as long as I'm already certain of the one whose image I'm bearing, if I'm certain of His thoughts about those hundreds of minutes in my day that no one else sees.

But it's all subtly destructive when I scan these images and fail to turn my eyes back to God. They too often become a checklist of all the ways I am less than: less than organized, less than responsible, less than spiritual, less than athletic, less than beautiful.

We become what we behold. When we're eager to mimic or to catalogue what we're missing, the way out isn't in internal chastisement or creating a rigorous self-improvement plan. The escape hatch is in where we set our eyes. God invites us to turn our eyes back to Him, to bear His image.

God is not just the creator of beauty. He is beauty itself. We become what we behold, and that beauty swells within us whenever we choose to behold Him.

I imagine that even though the jar of perfumed oil Mary wore around her neck was tightly sealed, it still released a fragrance. I picture her warming the bottle between her palms and holding it close, tracing the seal with her fingers, inhaling even the faintest whiff of scent.

Mary herself may have been something like that sealed container. Perhaps she kept her heart just as locked, doling out only small fragments of herself to friends and family.

Until she met Jesus.

As she had grown to know Him, she wanted only to know Him more and to be known by Him. She wanted to be like

Him, and she wanted to give Him more of what she'd tucked away to keep safe from others.

On the night her trembling hands broke the neck of the flask, her senses awakened. This woman whose days knew duty and practicality, sat in awe, enraptured. Her heart raced in love as the smell of the pungent oil, no longer a trace scent, enveloped her. Flooded her. Extravagance seeped from one room into the entire house.

The exchange was intimate and ravishing, rich for the senses of any who had eyes for what was truly happening as this woman gave herself away in the breaking of her jar, as she not only saw beauty from a distance but imbibed it.

She adored Him with the oil, with her hair unkempt. He was now even more beautiful to her. And she was becoming her true self as she moved nearer to Him.

Everyone there inhaled the anointing. All present could choose to look at Him—humbly radiant—or at her and at each other, criticizing her wasteful choice.

But her eyes were only on Jesus.

I'd barely sat down in the reading nook off to the side of our bedroom when I paused to look out the glass doors that open to our back porch and yard. The sky was suddenly aflame with color. Auburn with streaks of burnt gold illuminated my back yard, making silhouettes out of my favorite trees. I'm so unfamiliar with our landscape at dusk that I actually gasped when I saw it.

Most days as the sun goes down, I'm catering a meal for several voracious eaters or corralling children into pajamas and beds. But on this particular night, Nate had taken the kids to basketball practice and I'd tucked myself away, enjoying the stillness that fell on the house after the flurry of tying shoes and snatching water bottles and shoveling in "one more bite."

For the five minutes it took the sun to fall, I was rapt. Tearful, even. *You painted the sky for me*, I whispered to remind myself. And to acknowledge Him, because this was His doing.

His love notes are stashed everywhere. Every day in my back yard, there is a sunset. Every day in my back yard, there is riveting beauty. God's beauty is made for beholding. For *receiving.*

"If you want true beauty, look into the face of Jesus," writes preacher Charles Spurgeon.[6] Beauty is in the lines of His face, the humanity He wore for you and for me. But we tend to be a people of quick glances—even with God. Life at warp speed allows for little beholding. We are increasingly accustomed to three-minute waits and one-click purchases. And in our approach to God, we follow the same pattern. We want the soundbites. Or we wait in expectation for barked, impersonal orders. Or we expect to barrel through life and then sit down for thirty minutes and somehow find focus, though our hearts were racing for the other twenty-three and a half hours of our day. We want to gaze on God's beauty, we want to look into Jesus' face, but speed and beauty rarely coexist.

Hidden seasons invite us to slow down, to notice the beauty too often blurred by hurry, to cultivate the same wonder a toddler experiences watching a butterfly for the first time. Life's "little things"—the sunset behind the winter treeline, the flock of geese in perfect formation overhead, the aspens blazing in fall, the chicken-scratched love note left by a spouse under the coffeepot—all of these are mere reflections of another beauty. "God had created lower things to be signs that pointed to higher spiritual realities," writes George Marsden of Jonathan Edwards' perception of reality. "The universe, then, was a complex language of God. Nothing in it was accidental. Everything pointed to a higher meaning."[7] That we so often miss them reveals that we're also missing beauty in His truest form: Jesus.

Whether or not we are in a hidden season, whether or not we are in a busy season, we have to pause long enough to *look*. This look is not a passive look. Looking at God's beauty increases our desire for more of Him. It can grow our desire to look again. And again.

When we approach God with an open, mindful, hungry heart, we position ourselves not only to see His beauty but to let it change us.

I got a glimpse of God's beauty when Hope was baptized—submerged in water, wearing a dress over her bathing suit, exposed and still hidden as she told a dozen sets of eyes that she'd given her life to Jesus. I inhaled on that Sunday afternoon, receiving that this child and her life rested more deeply in God's grip than I had assessed.

I saw God's beauty when Lily leaped out of the car that brought her to our guest home in Uganda and squealed, "Daddy!" as she looked at her father's face, in person, for the first time. That night I lifted my eyes away from the fear of how this adoption might turn sour. Seeing a glimpse of what God was doing in it all infused faith into me.

I saw God's beauty on the day Nate proposed to me, and on the day, months earlier, when I knew I would marry that boy. I never thought I wanted the kind of love Nate offered. It threatened me and often caused me to retreat. But God showed me He knew my needs better than I did when I took time to look at the beauty behind this boy's pursuit of me.

I saw God's beauty in the countenance of a rough-worn teenager who bowed her heart to the love of God for the first time. In pausing to look in, as much as I could as an outsider, I started to believe that His beauty could overshadow any darkness.

I saw God's beauty in the lunar eclipse last night, on which millions of eyes were fixed. And that look changes me when I realize there is a Creator behind it, inviting me to see His creation and Himself as the best investment of my eyes.

But it's harder for me to see God's beauty late in the afternoon, in the thousands of minutes in the middle of my days that don't seem worthy of photographing or scrapbooking or sharing with others. He tells us in His Word that His glory is ever available, and it's tucked inside every day. Every single one.

The heavens declare the glory of God,
    and the sky above proclaims his handiwork.
Day to day pours out speech,
    and night to night reveals knowledge.
There is no speech, nor are there words,
    whose voice is not heard.

Their voice goes out through all the earth,
and their words to the end of the world.

—PSALM 19:1–4 ESV

It's my eyes that need training to see it in the middle minutes.

Too often, we relegate things like silence and wonder to others, such as monks or poets—the naturally contemplative, the ones we consider either social misfits or spiritual giants. We assume that these quiet, hidden times with God aren't for the extroverts, the social, the normal. We aren't that kind of odd or that kind of deep, and so we just don't go there, as if spending time looking long at God is only for weird loners or spiritual superheroes.

But when we cut ourselves off from attending to God in the quiet and the small, we're cutting ourselves off from soul food, starving ourselves of our life source, which is the unconventional sitting at His feet and seeing Him throughout every messy, wonder-filled moment of our day. We choose wonder when we look at God and talk with Him—even, and maybe especially, at the odd times. Author and pastor Eugene Peterson writes, "In prayer we intend to leave the world of anxieties and enter a world of wonder. We decide to leave an ego-centered world and enter a God-centered world. We will to leave a world of problems and enter a world of mystery. But it is not easy. We are used to anxieties, egos and problems; we are not used to wonder, God and mystery."[8]

Wonder means cracking open our eyes to see God, who is seeing us, *all the time.*

But wonder is sometimes shy. It slips the notice of hearts that refuse to look for it in the minutia of life.

Thus, God hides us.

Yes, even after the family skirmish and the flat tire and the visit to the doctor's office for the third time in one week—all things no one outside our world would know about—God calls us to wonder. We can ask Him to speak to us, then. We can find life in His Word, then. We can reach for His nearness, then. A life trained toward scanning the day for His wonders at *those* times is a life sinking its roots, strong, into love.

The moon has become our nightlight. The children are in bed, but not asleep. I open and close the front door with my hand on the latch so little ears can't hear.

I slide out into the evening, slippered, blanketed by a blue sky fading into dark black. I pad slowly around the circular drive in front of our house. I relish the quiet and the walls that separate me from the hum of the dishwasher, the rumble of the dryer, and the mindless thumps of Caleb's feet against the wall as he lies on his back and reads in bed.

I start praying, my insides filling the quiet with internal noise. I'm now both talking to God and listening to myself. It's never simple to get quiet.

After a few laps around our circular drive, I notice something, hear something I'd missed when my mind was still full from the day.

The crickets are loud, a synchrony to their hum. Something else is buzzing. I turn my head to listen. *What else in creation is awake at 8:00 p.m.?*

I hear movement on the hardened crabgrass that edges the woods—deer or coyotes, perhaps. And then an owl hoots in the far distance. The breeze picks up and the leaves skitter, awakened from their dormancy, and make their presence known. In some ways, the night outside is louder than dinnertime inside my home. There is a world out here, refusing to be quiet, refusing to be still and rest.

I smirk. I understand that kind of refusal. Cacophony is the soundtrack for my days. Even the nondescript parts of my day make noise. There is the constant buzz from the dryer producing piles of laundry that needs to be folded, the squeals and hollers of giddy children, and even the background hum of ocean waves from the white-noise machine in the upstairs bedroom—we often forget to turn it off, even when no one is asleep.

Quiet doesn't just happen. Ever.

Not even out here.

Internal stillness takes practice. It is the fruit of hiddenness—a life that's lived looking at God, a life of wonder in Him—and it needs to be cultivated.

Our fast-paced culture, our growing connectivity to friends all over the country, our endless to-do lists, and sometimes even the quietest of nights that allow for our unfettered and weighty thoughts to get loud oppose the communion that makes our hearts grow wildly deep. Perhaps all that goes against our calling to gaze at God's beauty only reinforces the need to look for it.

Elizabeth Barrett Browning says it aptly in her epic poem "Aurora Leigh":

> Earth's crammed with heaven,
> And every common bush afire with God:
> But only he who sees, takes off his shoes,
> The rest sit round it, and pluck blackberries.

Only those who see this beauty of His tucked within the ordinary are able to receive it as holy.

God loves to interrupt our days with Himself. He is always speaking, calling us back to our senses—back to what truly makes us come alive—inviting us to pause long enough to turn our eyes His way.

When my daughter Eden shouts from the yard on a busy afternoon, "It's a dove!" I peek out from the upstairs window to see a bird perched on our front walk, and something inside me stirs. A hummingbird that could fit inside my palm hovers over my zinnias out front, and the routine spin of my day stops. The sun catches Bo's hair as he looks up at Nate, and in that sweet, ordinary moment, I feel God call me to attention with this whispered love note.

I didn't always notice these things. I noticed birds when they left droppings on my car, and trees when their leaves clogged my gutters. They were things that needed my tending, my cleaning, my managing. The sunrise in the early morning blinded me on my morning run, and dusk was merely a transition to bedtime.

God was speaking, but I was too busy tasking to listen.

But when God hid me in difficult circumstances and the misunderstandings of others and within the confines of what many would call the mundane, I had time to notice these stealthily planted love notes. I began to see Him speaking with more than just instructions for good Christian living.

He wanted my affection, not my work. My willing lean into surrender.

The heavens were declaring the glory and the wonder and the beauty of God, and in these hidden seasons, I was aware that the deepest craving of my heart was to see Him. Everywhere.

Two years ago, I entered a season with a new baby and a new book, both needing my time and focused attention. It was in the midst of the flurry of responding to these needs that I realized I was waiting for life to somehow slow down so I could fully engage with God. Sure, I gave Him my time, but my mind and my heart weren't all there. I wasn't fully present with Him.

I had a mental list of things we'd talk about, God and me, when I finally had time to rest. I wasn't ignoring the need to rest before God and sit at His feet. Instead, I was working hard to get there. Once all the items on my list were checked off, I'd be in. I was looking at spending time with God as something that happened when all the work of life was complete, not something I could choose right in the middle of barreling through it.

So I instituted what I called my "wonder hour." In the midst of tending to my children's growing needs and book publicity and piles of winter laundry—extra socks and coats and gloves, every single week—I started to carve out time to wonder, to look at God.

I wrote "wonder hour" into slots on my calendar several times a week. This time was separate from my morning quiet time, and right in the middle of when I could be otherwise productive. And I did it as a way to make my schedule say what my heart wanted to say: *Jesus, sitting at Your feet is never a waste of time.* During wonder hour, I chose to trust God with a part of my life I clung to most tightly: my time.

I closed the bedroom door, hung an antique brown key on the handle to signal to all the little people on the other side of the door that I was not to be disturbed, and I opened my mind to God. Some days I read the Psalms, and other days the gospels. Some days I read poetry that lifted my eyes to Him or a book that might stir me toward a greater understanding of His hand in my life.

I said with my schedule, *You, God, are the best thing I have going today.* My to-do list might be stymied, but my wonder hour was a concrete way for me to hide myself in God, to choose holy wonder over productivity. It was a reach toward surrendering my story to God by surrendering my schedule and squandering my time—with Him.

I still schedule wonder hours into my weeks, and it still isn't easy. I have to fight for it. The days are full. And when I say fight, I mean the battle that goes on inside myself. It always seems a lot easier to tackle grocery shopping for the week than it does to settle quietly into conversation with God. But one movement in that direction, no matter how small (even ten minutes), creates a pathway for wonder over time. As life gets even more full—more laundry, more "can I lie across your bed and talk to you, Mommy?" minutes, more ideas brewing to put on a page, more friends in deep need—I am continuing, ever so slowly, to pattern my life toward what I first began to learn when I canceled plans to cry over my Bible after yet another baby shower: tucked away in a hidden place, looking to God is what brings me back to life.

Still in the fog of morning sluggishness and with a thinly veiled air of motherly annoyance, I dropped my four older children at soccer practice with water bottles and balls and snacks in baggies. I thought perhaps I could use a few laps around a field to clear my head. So I put two-year-old Bo in the stroller with no plan for where to walk, just knowing I needed to pound it out on the pavement. The chaotic early morning rush to get everyone ready and out the door had shredded my nerves. I struggled to like my kids in that single moment, and I surely didn't like myself. I was remembering why we didn't do these early morning activities very often.

On days like this, I have to whittle life down to one passage, which is part of training my eyes to see wonder: "On the glorious splendor of your majesty, and on your wondrous works, I will meditate. They shall speak of the might of your awesome deeds, and I will declare your greatness" (Ps. 145:5–6 ESV).

I pushed and pounded harder than necessary to move the stroller, but with as much exertion as I needed to work out the morning's frustrations. I recited these verses in my head a dozen times while replaying the last forty-five minutes of trying to hustle everyone out the front door. The flustered child whose water bottle didn't have as much ice as she wanted. The missing shin guard. The squealing baby and the car seat stained from last week's takeout that I'd forgotten to clean.

Then this one phrase interrupted my venting: "I will declare your greatness."

The morning wasn't great. They were grumpy. I was terse. They were late. I was unforgiving. They joined a field of players who had lily-white skin and families that from the outside certainly looked more intact than ours. This morning held so much more than soccer, and very little of it was great by my standards. But I would find Him, here.

Is this a time to reach back and remember? I wondered. *To declare the greatness of the God who hurdled mountains of paperwork impossibilities to bring our children home? The God who brought them today onto a soccer field with breakfast in their bellies and a mommy who would ask their forgiveness when practice was over? The God who made this toddler in the stroller in front of me, after my womb was empty for twelve years?*

A small flash of color on the path caught my eye, and I swerved the wheels of the stroller to miss a brilliant blue eggshell.

"Look, Bo!" I said pointing, still halfway lost in my thoughts. "A birdie was in that egg!"

"Egg. Egg. Eggie!" Bo's voice grew louder with each repetition. I set my feet back on the path and my mind back on the Psalms: "On the glorious splendor of your majesty, and on your wondrous works, I will meditate . . . I will declare your greatness."

With each phrase of the passage, the erratic pounding of my heart was recalibrating, finding its steady rhythm again. I was telling my soul what was true as if it were undergoing CPR. The morning still felt messy. I was relieved our long-term houseguest hadn't witnessed my behavior, and I didn't really want to tell Nate about it later. But I did want to repent to my children. I had spent long years without ever asking for forgiveness from Nate in our early married days, so my desire to repent was significant. God was doing a work in me.

As we continued on the path, Bo intermittently interrupted my thoughts with "Oh!" pointing in childlike wonder to a tree and then a car and back at the eggshell as we passed it on our return trek. And now I couldn't seem to get my mind off it. This shell struck me as so much more than a discarded home for a baby bird. This small piece of God's created order evoked a question I'd been asking with my life but hadn't put into words until this morning: *What is greatness to You, God? What* are *Your wondrous works?*

I'd seen God's greatness in the miracle ruling in the Ugandan court system that granted two children a home in our family. My marriage is a wonder—we made it through the rise and fall of a business and the rise and fall of our stubborn hearts. My children, though I might have thought them ruffians that morning, were having parts of their broken hearts restored. All of these were glorious wonders.

But the eggshell. And the soccer practice down the street. Wonders?

God was inviting me to reconsider the ever-unfolding opportunities for wonder around me. There were opportunities for awe at God in even the most unlikely moments, and my eyes needed to be trained to see them as much as my heart needed to be trained to engage them. God was available, infused into my every minute, but my flesh was bent toward independence. I hadn't been trained to see Him in the eggshell. Or at soccer practice.

I could see the wonder of God in the knowing look Nate gave me across the kitchen island the night before when he heard me encouraging a child he knew would be easier for me to critique. I was in awe of God as my daughter, who has a painful history, slid her hand into mine at church while we sang, "I see heaven invading this place." I was invited to wonder later that day when I shut the door to my bedroom to ask Him for help with a different (presently difficult) child. He was wondrous when I didn't have time to text friends for prayer but paused to talk to Him in the midst of chaos and felt that permeating peace that could be attributed only to God. And wonder was in my children who were merely players on a field to most spectators of the game, but who were beginning to understand that they are a son and daughters when no one but God, Nate, and I are looking.

Yes, the eggshell and the soccer practice are wonders. These things are beautiful because they point to a Creator God who both sees and orchestrates the glorious details of life. Who reaches *into* my minutes. These things have the power to cause me to look at Him, if I step back and let them. They have the power to move my heart, if I let it engage.

Dozens of minutes every day are shot through with this wonder, pregnant with potential to draw our eyes up to God. Our flitting eyes, with just as many opportunities to behold things that won't nourish our souls, need to be trained to see them. They need to be trained to see the face of Jesus.

The house fills with the fragrance of oil. The whole earth fills with His glory. My soul fills with awareness of His wonder. Today.

And before long, I'm unwinding, sitting before Him in the small moments of the day, sliding my watch off my wrist and looking up to Him alone.

For Your Continued Pursuit

Genesis 1:26–27 | 1 Kings 19:11–12 | Psalm 5:3 | Psalm 16:8 | Psalm 17:6 | Psalm 19:1–4 | Psalm 27:4 | Psalm 45:10–11 | Psalm 65:1 | Psalm 81:10 | Psalm 139:1–6, 16–18 | Psalm 145:5–6 | Song of Songs 2:14 | Isaiah 55:1–2 | Hosea 6:6 | Matthew 6:22 | Luke 22:39–45 | John 11:28–37 | 2 Corinthians 3:18 | 2 Corinthians 4:16–18 | 2 Corinthians 10:12

seven

SECRET EXTRAVAGANCE

Wasting Ourselves on God

"Why this waste?"
—MATTHEW 26:8

I'd been in a suit and heels since 5:00 a.m., and after a full morning, I was at the airport for an early afternoon flight home—home to a husband, but no children. It was a couple of years after my season at the boutique on North Barracks Road, but still a few years before the grief of infertility had settled into my soul.

I'd recently started to crave *more*. I wanted more from my sales support job. I wasn't tired of doing it or even tired of the deskwork and the travel, but I was tired of working for little more than sales goals and a paycheck. I wanted more than productivity and success. I wanted brushes with God and meaning and almost anything that mattered but wasn't easily measured.

My work for the day was done and I was tired, but my heart was hungry, and I was beginning to like heart hunger. So I prayed: *God, I want to meet with You in this airport.*

Meeting Him required quieting my insides enough to hear and respond. The kind of dialogue I was learning to have with God burgeoned when I saw it as an exchange—my mind for His thoughts, my fear for His assurance, my whispers for His response. As I made my way to a restaurant near my gate, I noticed an elderly gentleman who was being pushed in a wheelchair. I prayed for God to breathe life and strength into his frail body. I saw a man running as fast as my mind usually worked, and I prayed his racing heart would come to know Jesus. I saw a young woman with vacant eyes, and I prayed she would find the filling her heart most needed. I realized afresh that the people all around me weren't merely interesting. They were God-created. I wanted to talk to Him about what He had made.

God, what do You see in the man who is late for his flight? And the one in the wheelchair—how do You see the heart buried underneath that broken body? Rather than looking at people as faces among the masses, I asked for His eyes for them and responded with minute-long prayers: *God, I want to meet You in this airport.*

No one knew this conversation I was having in my head with God. And I was starting to like these secret exchanges.

At the restaurant, I grabbed the last available seat at the bar, which was full of day travelers with carry-ons. As I scooted up onto my stool and glanced at the laminated menu, I noticed the gentleman sitting next to me. He looked to be near retirement, but he was dressed for business. I was drawn to him in the way you're drawn to someone who is not at all like you, but with whom you feel a strange connection.

Maybe I'm supposed to share the gospel with this man, I thought. I ordered my food and opened my book, trying to concentrate on reading while staying aware of what felt like a nudge from God.

Ten minutes later when the waitress brought out my order along with that of the man next to me, I noticed that we both had ordered the same meal. I awkwardly mumbled a comment about it, looking for a way to begin a conversation. But my voice, perhaps too quiet from nerves, got lost in a salvo of loudspeaker announcements. He hadn't heard me. I went back to my book, resigned that I'd misread God's cues.

The book I was reading explored the concept of abiding in the vine from John 15. The author used the notion of tree grafting to illustrate this abiding. After hours of client presentations on throbbing feet, my mind couldn't absorb the words. I read and reread the same paragraph, but without comprehension. And then this prompt dropped into my mind: *Ask the man sitting next to you to explain it.*

Uh-oh, I thought.

As much as I wanted to hear from God, I knew that we humans sometimes mishear Him and mistake our mental wanderings for His voice. *What should I do?* Talk to the man and risk awkwardness and embarrassment? Or not talk to him and risk missing what might well be God's answer to my prayer to meet with Him in this airport?

Well, at least I'll never see this guy again, I thought. So I went for it.

"Sir, excuse me," I said, much louder this time, almost shouting to compensate for my nerves.

He startled. "Yes?" he said, raising his eyebrows like the authoritative boss of a fresh college grad.

"Do you know anything about grafting?" I coughed out.

"What?" he asked.

Oh no. I had to say it again. This business exec didn't even seem to know what the word meant.

"Grafting, sir. Do you know anything about grafting?" My face was red hot.

"It's funny you should ask," he said. I noticed tears welling up in the corners of his eyes.

My heart started racing.

"I majored in agriculture in college and I minored in grafting. I run a farm equipment business but have gotten away from what I once loved."

Now I was sure I could actually hear my heart, not just feel the pounding.

He stretched back on his stool, took off his glasses, and rubbed his eyes. Then he enthusiastically explained the details of how the branch of one tree is grafted into another as if he were telling me a page-turning story. I showed him the paragraph in my book and asked him questions. He made it all so clear.

I'm not sure if I was more surprised that the prompt to talk to this man really was from God, or that God was personal enough to meet me at an airport barstool. Apparently, God was meeting this man too, right over his hamburger and French fries. He thanked me after our exchange as if he'd been reminded of his boyish love for trees and for grafting, a love that needed rediscovering.

Twelve years later, this conversation remains my most memorable business trip. Still, I can't remember where I'd gone or even who I met with on that trip. I remember it only because I'd felt seen and heard by God.

God showed up when I was in my suit and heels, and He winked. We shared a secret. During those days of client presentations, excel spreadsheets, and conference calls, He was whispering, *I want to meet with you, here.* What I might once have considered a waste of time—conversation with Him in the midst of a demanding day—became, instead, food for my hungry heart. It was a gift of hiddenness during a season when my work required me to be on during the workday.

God's currency is communion—a relationship that *grows*, nearer still. A relationship that is cultivated when no one else is looking. A relationship accessed not just when we feel we need His help but at all the odd times that punctuate our agenda-driven days. A depth of relationship that feeds the recipient in the way that productivity and accomplishment just cannot.

What a waste. What a beautiful waste.

"Why this waste?" A condemnation wrapped in a question. It is among the most powerful lines in Mary's story, spoken by onlookers as she poured a fortune on Jesus' feet. She'd grown accustomed to the scornful looks of the religious leaders, but these bystanders were Jesus' friends—their condemnation perhaps, then, more jarring for her.

But Mary had been here before, frustrating those who valued her productivity over her passion. She had already been chastised by her sister, Martha, for wasting time at Jesus' feet, but Jesus had praised Mary's choice. She'd found what mattered. And she was developing a habit of this, uncapping her love and offending those who couldn't handle the waste.

"Why this waste?" they asked. Their words shielded them from an expression of love they likely feared as well as craved. They too had been close to Jesus. They'd known there was something wildly different about this man, but they apparently were trapped in an old standard of measurement that dismissed devotion like this as waste. Now that she'd shown what she valued most, everyone knew she was different. Surely such extravagance must be a waste. After all, what would she have to show for it?

Wasteful. By their standards.

Precious. By His.

"Wherever this gospel is preached in the whole world," Jesus said, "what this woman has done will also be told as a memorial to her" (Matt. 26:13). Jesus acclaimed Mary's choice then, and He invites us to make the same choice now: to live by a reckless love—even, and perhaps especially, in our hiddenness.

Extravagant, hidden giving to Jesus at the expense of publicly productive Christian service will always offend. Yes, even Christians. Yet it is all over the Word of God. Read these verses with an eye for this uncorked, abandoned, and extravagant love that happens perhaps even at the expense of producing something for Him:

> LORD, I have loved the habitation of Your house, and the
> place where Your glory dwells. (Ps. 26:8)

His house is rich. It's where He is. Stay there for just a little while longer than you're used to and, over time, it will no longer feel strange to orient your schedule around being in that place.

> One thing I have desired of the LORD, that will I seek:
> that I may dwell in the house of the LORD all the days
> of my life. (Ps. 27:4)

When we cross over to heaven, we won't discover a new, mysterious craving for God. It is here that we practice. We cultivate. We are made for this: to waste time simply being with Him. Sitting at His feet enjoying him isn't a foolish expenditure of time. It's strength training for heaven.

> But one thing is needed, and Mary has chosen that
> good part, which will not be taken away from her.
> (Luke 10:42)

Jesus said this about a woman who chose to forfeit productivity and to risk judgment to sit with Him and learn from Him.

> You shall love the LORD your God with all your heart,
> with all your soul, and with all your strength. (Deut. 6:5)

Hiddenness turns dutiful workers into lovers of God. To stay in love, we must resist the culture. To resist the culture, we must stay in love. Author Henri Nouwen says it this way: "The farther I run away from the place where God dwells, the less I am able to hear the voice that calls me the Beloved, and the less I hear that voice, the more entangled I become in the manipulations and power games of the world."[9]

At some point it became an easy decision for Mary to pour out her life savings on Jesus' feet. To surrender herself there. She didn't do it out of guilt or obligation. She did it out of a wildly extravagant love.

She was *wastefully* in love.

A decade and a half after my summer at the camp in the Adirondacks, the routine of my mothering days hasn't changed all that much. It is just as patterned and just as circular. Wake, prepare breakfast, clean up breakfast, prepare lunch, clean up lunch, plan for dinner. Set the table for several hungry bodies, clear the table. Reset. The same pair of Eden's jeans goes from worn to washed to folded to worn multiple times in a week. We empty the diaper bin on the same day the next shipment of diapers arrives.

Some might use a word like trapped to describe such an existence. I confess there are some weak days I might be tempted to also.

Tears of former orphans fall and hearts move ever so slightly and the babe learns a new word—all in the eight hours that no one else sees. But these are just the little minutes between long hours of sweeping floors and turning off lights and tying shoes and wiping up drool.

Is this all there is? pokes at me.

My day might look different from yours, but I suspect the same question haunts you.

At twenty-two, before children, I was telling high school students—future world-changers—about Jesus. Stories of transformed lives made the long summer hours in the dining hall and weekday afternoons of ministry administration worth it. My life had purpose, purpose I could measure one life at a time.

Today, with six children, I could coach myself in the same way and find the stories that make the tedium worth it. That point in the afternoon when I catch my little girl at the piano writing a song from her Bible makes me think, *Something besides diapers is being changed around here. At least I'm not wasting my time.* When I see four of them, with different histories of brokenness, spread out on their backs on the trampoline laughing between fits of jumping and squealing, I forget how long it took to prepare their dinner.

Maybe you do the same. We scout our days, you and me, for these stories that make it all worth it. We're forever on the lookout for new ways to infuse our otherwise mundane lives with measurable impact. We troll for tiny signs that what we're doing matters, a mark on the earth, whether in the glowing successes of our children or the business promotion or the ministry we launched. Parenting feels most like it's worth it when we see our child thrive, and the business or ministry seems to most warrant our outpouring when it's growing.

But what if our real mark on earth was meant to reverberate in heaven? What if there is a possibility for impact—impacting God's heart with our hidden devotion to Him—that far supersedes these this-made-it-all-worth-it moments?

The mundane hours can outweigh the one this-made-it-all-worth-it moment in a week if we are meeting God and pouring ourselves out at His feet, there. What if right in the middle of that mundanity we could *waste*? Like Mary at Jesus' feet.

Without a vision for what's available to us in sitting at His feet in the hidden place, we become restless. This restlessness is powerful enough to make us start new projects, sign up to volunteer, begin foundations, delve into new ministries. Many a small group is launched, blog written, and book published by ones who are itching to climb out of the hidden place. All these things can be beautiful within God's timing. But out of time, they will only perpetuate the restlessness, the craving for the next "soul hit." We become thrill seekers who miss the biggest thrill. We train ourselves to be satisfied with so little.

And so God whispers to us, *Don't climb out of this hidden, mundane place*—don't start the foundation, run after a new ministry, defend yourself to your critics, start the next blog—*just yet. Find Me. Here.*

Every single minute of the day is available for us to feel His hand resting, firmly, on the small of our backs and His breath brushing like a breeze against our skin, softly awakening us. His beauty is close, disruptively near.

Every single minute is available for wasting ourselves at His feet. To reach the dwelling place, to see and know Him there, we need to allow for the quiet, the questions. We need to lean into, and not away from, what can come out of the aching hiddenness with God.

We've been sequestered.

The closet, the corner, the place where we've been hidden from the crowd is where God's whisper becomes a life-changing brush with His love. All the waiting rooms in life, the wasteful places where the only question is, "When will I ever get out of this place?" are the places God loves to show us Himself.

The waste of extravagant love we pour at Jesus' feet is never squandered. That love expands us, it doesn't diminish us. We weren't made to ration our love. We were made for extravagance.

For Your Continued Pursuit

Deuteronomy 4:29 | Deuteronomy 6:5 | Psalm 26:8 | Psalm 27:4 | Psalm 41:12 | Psalm 119:130–32 | Proverbs 8:17 | Jeremiah 9:23–24 | Matthew 6:33 | Matthew 26:8–9 | Luke 10:39–42 | John 12:43 | Galatians 1:10 | Ephesians 3:17–19 | Colossians 3:23

eight

THE NEEDS AROUND US

Changing the World at Jesus' Feet

"For this fragrant oil might have been
sold for much and given to the poor."

—MATTHEW 26:9

The earth is still covered in night, but I am waking. I hit the snooze button on the alarm for just a few more moments of rest, but my mind is already racing into the day, dragging with it the missed opportunities from the day before.

I think of a woman we bump into from time to time. An adult orphan and still without family, she is in need of more than just an occasional conversation and a smile. *Should I have invited her over for dinner when I saw her yesterday?*

I had skimmed a blog post on the plight of Syrian refugees: *Should we open our home?*

I remember a neighbor's brother who is in the hospital: *Someone else is coordinating meals for them. Should that have been me?*

I had received a text image of a child in foster care: *We have one extra bedroom. Should we adopt again?*

The needs are unending. And all before breakfast. All before even getting out of bed.

I have time and resources and the world has needs. Isn't this an equation with only one correct answer: me?

My resources are at God's disposal. He may sometimes ask me to take a risk to meet those needs, to do more than I think I can. But I err when I think of resources, whether time, money, or spikenard oil, as merely transactional. As if meeting needs alone is the only thing, or the most important thing, God desires of me. If meeting needs is my primary focus, I've missed a foundational step: friendship with the King. To meet any need, I first have to hear God's whisper about that need.

"No longer do I call you servants," Jesus said to his followers, "for a servant does not know what his master is doing; but I have called you friends, for all things that I heard from My Father I have made known to you" (John 15:15).

Friends talk. They share hearts and get their fingernails dirty in one another's stories. They carry the load for the other. And sometimes they are simply present.

We often assume that God, however, is somehow pining away for just one thing: our A+ effort so this broken world can *finally* be fixed. As if He is anxiously waiting to see which one of us will respond and how well we will do. We make our relationship with Him transactional. We give, He gives in return. We mess up, He withholds His love from us.

We make our worth dependent on our ability to meet

the needs around us. And when we're honest about the darker parts of our hearts, we have to admit our actions for others can sometimes be an attempt to feel good about all we can do for God.

But to a friend, time is an investment of the heart, not just the hand.

Friends spend. Time.

Every day I am flooded by opportunities to change the world by meeting the needs around me. Any servant can meet a need, but what about sons and daughters? Do beloved children exchange chores for room and board or even for affection? Or how would parents respond to children who gladly cleaned the house and mowed the lawn but refused to spend time talking with and enjoying them, the very ones who have loved and cared for them their whole lives? We know this isn't the way things should operate in a healthy family, and yet we often and subconsciously relate to God in this way. We give Him what we perceive to be our obedience yet internally resist a deeper surrender.

On any day, I am overwhelmed by the needs of the world, but my greater need is to interrupt this kneejerk cycling between the cries of the world and my response so that I can cultivate friendship with God. It's there that I learn that it's the friends of God who truly change the world. It's there that I have the depth of friendship that informs the way I respond to the world's needs.

When I let friendship with God become my first priority—talking to Him, hearing from Him, letting His Word shape my thinking—I align myself with an agenda that does, in fact, help meet the needs of others. But instead of being driven by my limited cost–benefit analysis, I get to tap into the wisdom of the greatest king of the earth and heavens. And as I scoot nearer to Him, my senses are awakened. I move from being an efficient and productive worker to a friend who can touch and see and engage with God. I grow to love the things and the people He loves—with my actions, with my time, and with my presence.

Lovers will always outwork workers.

As Mary did with her fragrant oil, I want to spend myself on Jesus. I want to move His heart with an extravagant out-pouring. The world changes from an exchange such as this. Instead of frantically scurrying to meet the latest need, I slowly pattern my life toward pouring myself out at His feet—toward giving Him the best of my affection, sometimes in a hundred small glances a day. It's from that place of connection that I hear His heartbeat for the needs around me and see His per-spective on my role. It's from there, that place of carrying His heart, that I learn how and when to respond to others' cries.

We're training for a lifetime of friendship with God, an eternity. Yet training and friendship may seem to be opposi-tional words. We train for road races and learning the piano and acquiring new job skills. We take parenting classes and computer classes. But friendship? Shouldn't that just *happen*?

Not exactly.

When transactional beings who live in a world focused on productivity meet a relational God, we *do* need training for how to settle into friendship with Him. Repatterning. Spending time with Him in hiddenness orients us toward that repatterning.

Responding to the needs of the world from the foundation of friendship with God takes practice. This is not natural to us, but it is possible for us. Here are some thoughts on how to grow toward what might not feel natural: friendship with God.

Look at Him first thing. Each day.

For me, training begins in the morning while I'm still in bed, even before the morning light splinters through my bedroom blinds, before I am subjected to the vulnerability that accompanies a fresh day. I am most raw in these transitional morning moments, just after waking from six or seven hours of sleep and dreams. Left unfettered, my morning thoughts are first populated by all the not-God voices clamoring for my attention, from my insecure heart's wanderings to a replay of a conversation from the day before to the thoughts about the latest needs of others who are right in front of me. Or sometimes my mind simply fixates on how I need a chai latte if I'm going to function at all.

But I've learned that the morning is for Him to hold—to hold me. I love these words from the psalmist: "My voice You shall hear in the morning, O LORD; in the morning I will direct it to You, and I will look up" (Ps. 5:3).

The morning is often when I feel most susceptible to the thoughts flying through my head. I could wake on the defensive, but God loves to receive my most vulnerable self.

For nearly a year, I woke up every single morning with the hymn "I Need Thee Every Hour" playing in my head, ushering me into alertness. It was as if God was reminding me I was *that* needy. I had masked my weaknesses for so long that it was freeing to finally admit—and first thing in the morning, almost as the pronouncement over my day—how much I needed God.

Now, whether or not I wake up with that hymn ringing in my ears, my first words nearly every morning are, "God, I need you." In the rawest, most vulnerable part of my day, I position myself as needy and attentive. I decide to listen to Him, to look at Him, rather than chase after the myriad things clamoring for my attention.

These are the gentle but intentional acknowledgments of friendship with God. Instead of settling for a transactional relationship, I see Him entering into the still, small minutes of my day. The almost undetectable moments. And I want Him there—not just because I need help but because I like His presence.

If I go for too long during the day—too many minutes of checking my email or padding through the house lost in thoughts or hanging out in anger over a scuffle with my children or with Nate—without anchoring what I see and how I see it in biblical truth, the day shows it, and I wear it. I am anxious, the clamor of needs around me speaks louder than His voice, and circumstantial peace becomes my goal. So instead, I learn from my toddler how to be like a child.

My toddler, Bo, sweetly warm in his footie pajamas as he wakes up, can't quite rip through the house with his normal confidence until I've held him close, read him a few stories, and combed my fingers through his bed-worn hair. I'm the same way with my heavenly Father. I need to be held, to be weak, to be secure in the arms of someone who loves me no matter what the day brings. I need to be cuddled. I wake vulnerable, and I want to give that vulnerability to Him.

I give Him my best affection. First.

And my roots go down.

Give yourself permission to start where you are and to start small.

One year when I was in full-time ministry, our staff team set aside an entire January day for prayer. We piled into cars, drove a few hours to a retreat center, and spent the day fasting and praying for the lives of high school students and their families.

We scattered ourselves throughout the cavernous meeting room, carving out our own spaces to ask God to move in and through the people He'd put in our lives and ministry. Hour by hour, the topic for prayer changed. We knelt. We stood with arms raised. We huddled in groups and then walked the outside perimeter of the building, breathing into our hands to keep them warm. With our hearts and our bodies, including our empty stomachs, we wanted to say to God, *We seek You first for this ministry.*

It was an intense and memorable day, but perhaps not in the way it should have been for me. What I remember most was my apathy and agitation.

I was restless, checking my watch after an hour. My body wasn't used to fasting and my mind wasn't used to praying for one hour, much less the long hours of an entire day. I felt like a junior varsity cross-country runner at the Olympics.

I knew prayer is the real work of God, but I couldn't cut it. I didn't fit here. I was bored, and God felt distant, all while my stomach grumbled.

I guess I'm more cut out for the actual work of God, not the conversation with Him, I decided as I glanced around at my teammates, who mostly seemed engrossed in prayer and not hungry at all.

For years after that day, when something came up about an extended period of prayer, I told myself, *Some people can pray a lot and some can't. I'm one of the ones who can't*. My mind kept going back to that day of being bored and distracted and indifferent.

A decade later, I was tucking Lily into bed and kissing her cheek, silently breathing a prayer: *God, heal this broken heart of hers*. I had four children, and spending a day, much less an hour, in prayer wasn't planned for the next week or the next year. The next day, I'd be doing laundry and clearing dishes and facing exactly what I'd faced that day—the same hurdles of being a tired mom with more needs than I could meet.

But at that point in my life, my minute-long prayers were multiplying, consistently and covertly escorting me into longer conversations with God, conversations that were moving beyond my morning quiet time and into the parts of my day where I was most inclined to produce something.

I remembered that long-ago January day of extended prayer, and it made more sense to me why I couldn't spend the focused time with God that seemed to come so easily to others in that room. A full day of conversation with God—at a time when my mind was oriented toward impact and God was my coach, not someone I wanted to be with—was too intangible to my immature heart. I wasn't there yet. I had eyes for ministry impact and related to God as the one coaching me to get there, not as someone I wanted to spend time with and enjoy. And so He was unfamiliar to me, a mere acquaintance.

But somewhere between that January day and the night of my breath prayer for Lily, I had begun relating to God as a friend. Slowly, imperceptibly, I'd moved from seeing Him as a coach who constantly pushed me to work harder, to seeing Him as a loving Father who wants to share His heart with me. As a result, my conversations with God changed from once-a-day requests for help with tasks and assignments, to moment-to-moment breath prayers throughout my day. A string of tiny prayers. This is how you talk to friends, after all: frequently and openly.

And so I became more intentional about those tiny prayers. I prayed phrases of Scripture up the stairs and down, chopping onions, walking to the mailbox. I allowed myself to make small requests as well as big ones, reminding myself that God cares just as much about this one ordinary moment as He does the big moments.

Strengthen me on my insides, I prayed from Ephesians 3:16 when anxiety and fear clouded my thinking.

Open my eyes, that I may see wondrous things from your law, I prayed from Psalm 119:18, especially when His Word felt more like a textbook to me than the love letter my eyes had read dozens of times. I wanted a new start the next day.

Create in me a clean heart, O God, I prayed from Psalm 51:10

when I was terse with my children and grumpy about my lot in life.

Other days it was, *Lord, please change her heart,* over a child's attitude. Or, *Strengthen the weak parts of Nate,* rather than an internal complaint about him. Or, *Help her sleep, God,* as I closed the bedroom door after tucking Eden in.

I exchanged anxious thoughts—wondering what a friend thought of me, fearing the outcome of my children's behaviors, worrying about the unpaid bill—with tiny prayers from His Word. (He was beginning to infuse the minutia of my day.) I started these conversations just as I might initiate a conversation with a new friend. *Here's a tidbit about me. Tell me a little about You.*

Whereas my prayer life had once revolved around asking God for the big things—salvation for a teenager, funding for an adoption, greater impact for a ministry endeavor—now I was all about the small things. *God, I'm tired. Would You meet me in this exhaustion and lift me up?* Or, *I'm feeling overwhelmed by my list today. Would You bring me peace in this moment?*

Tiny prayers assume more of God than they do of us. They acknowledge that He is big enough to receive a small request and respond. He starts where we are, and sometimes we need to start small. In our footie pajamas, even. Childlike. And yet God always seems to respond with more than we even know to ask for. Through my tiny prayers, I noticed subtle growth, a new and fresh hunger for God. My tiny prayers were carving new space in my spirit to hear God's voice and to expect an enjoyable exchange, not a monologue.

When the needs of the world were clamoring loudly, I

could see these nascent, minute-by-minute reaches for God as a waste of time. Or I could see them as partnering with a Friend who can do exceedingly abundantly above all that I ask or imagine—through me and with me as we do life together.

Follow Jesus' example of being tethered to God.

Jesus talked to God.

The one who *was* God's image—made from God, carrying all of God, wearing the fullest expression of God in skin—talked to God.

Often.

- "Now in the morning, having risen a long while before daylight, He went out and departed to a solitary place; and there He prayed" (Mark 1:35).
- "But Jesus often withdrew to lonely places and prayed" (Luke 5:16 NIV).
- "In the days of his flesh, Jesus offered up prayers and supplications, with loud cries and tears, to him who was able to save him from death, and he was heard because of his reverence" (Heb. 5:7 ESV).

We so often approach prayer as mere discipline. While discipline is a starting place for conversation with God and a tool for those of us who need structure, discipline wasn't Jesus' foundation for communicating with God.

For Jesus, conversations with God began with desire, not discipline. He stayed close to God. Tethered.

They were already one—God and Jesus—united with the Spirit, and yet Jesus loved being with the Father, who loved

Him. Jesus invites us to share in this oneness with Him. He prayed this for us: "I do not pray for these alone, but also for those who will believe in Me through their word; that they all may be one, as You, Father, are in Me, and I in You; that they also may be one in Us, that the world may believe that You sent Me" (John 17:20–21).

Jesus prayed that our unity with God would be like His unity with God, born not of duty but of desire. Of friendship.

We get a small infusion of God—a spark of an idea, a dream that could impact the world around us, a nudge that might change circumstances—and we run with it without tracing it to its source. We believe that the work of God, in and through us, to meet the world's needs is the greatest demonstration of Him in our lives. Though that work is significant and often substantive, we can chase it with such fury that we miss the dozens of opportunities for friendship-like conversation with God along the way, for stillness to hear God's whispers as we work.

We feel the same discomfort with a story like Mary's that the others in the room did that night. Discomfort turns to judgment turns to dismissal—until we look at the concealed parts of our lives and acknowledge, *I feel better when I'm producing, and I feel best when it's noticed.*

Yet God continues to bring us back to friendship with Him and to the layered understanding of the motives behind our pursuits.

Jesus, whose assignment was to save the whole world, took time out to be with God. He regularly separated himself from the crowds and their needs—the unhealed bodies and the

144

leprous skin and the broken families—to communicate with His Father, His friend. And the Father didn't merely need the Son. The Father loved Him. Jesus said, "As the Father loved Me, I also have loved you" (John 15:9).

This is the kind of relationship, the love exchange, into which we are invited.

This kind of scoot-up-close-to-me-and-let-me-share-myself-with-you relationship isn't a quick burst of affection we're given so that we can do what God wants of us. It's a love that can seep into our core and change us if we look at Him and receive what He offers as He reaches back to us. Then we will see our families, our neighborhoods, our world with new eyes as He imparts more of Himself to us.

Speak the Word of God. Out loud.

I hadn't seen Nate pray the Word of God out loud like this before we got to Uganda.

We'd gone on an impulse, a strong nudge from the Lord, and spent money we didn't yet have, all in an effort to adopt two children that the Ugandan legal system might not even release to us. We were there for almost six weeks but had packed for months, unsure of when we might return.

These were the craziest days of our married life. Nate was enflamed with holy determination, and I was afraid. At a glance, the whole thing looked like a foolish crusade to save children who didn't yet know us and who might be even further scarred if the adoption process failed and fell apart, slaying their hopes. Our future was in the hands of an unfamiliar judge and a mostly unbending system.

We met with our lawyer in the lobby of our guest home.

He was pleasant, but frank. This didn't look good for us. He'd told us not to come, and we'd lived up to his expectations of irrational but determined Americans who hoped their dollars and good intentions would force circumstances to work their way. But here we were. The likelihood was high that we would soon return to the States, thousands fewer dollars in our pockets and without the children we longed to make our own.

So I lay awake at night under the mosquito net (which seemed to trap mosquitoes in, rather than keep them out) and obsessed about all the possible outcomes while Nate snored beside me. But in the mornings, he prayed. Bible in hand, he walked the perimeter of our guest home, speaking aloud the Word of God. I'd heard Nate teach the Bible and had seen him spend many mornings with his well-worn Bible open across his lap and a cup of coffee in his hand. But I hadn't heard him pray like this—out loud, as if he were preaching a sermon to himself.

Around he went: in front of the unruly and easily agitated watchdog, underneath the lines of laundry drying out back, and between the fence and the guardhouse. Again and again, morning after morning. For almost six weeks.

The judge's office was closing early this season, we learned.

Nate paced and prayed God's Word.

Two more pieces of paperwork were missing from our file.

Nate circled the house with his Bible in hand, his mouth open, preaching the Word back to himself.

No new verdict on our case on the day they promised to deliver it.

Around the guest home again.

"The words that I speak to you are spirit, and they are life" (John 6:63).

Before we went to Uganda, Nate and I had approached parts of God's Word as if they were merely platitudes and rules for clean living. They'd been moral guidelines—until we were desperate for them to be so much more.

When Nate began to speak the Word of God, our relationship to Scripture changed and deepened. These words and passages weren't edicts or codes of conduct handed down by a distant and intangible God. These words were living Truth, loving Truth, *the* Truth, and we mainlined every morsel as Nate spoke them around the guesthouse and into his heart.

As I watched Nate from the guesthouse window, I started saying under my breath the same words Nate was speaking as instigators for my own conversation with God. And with each passing day, I noticed a subtle shift. I wasn't just hearing these words preached, I was metabolizing them. They were life-giving food, nourishment for my roots in God's love.

The Word of God takes new shape when we don't just read it but *hear* it, and from our own mouths. "So then faith comes by hearing, and hearing by the word of God" (Rom. 10:17). *The Message* puts it this way: "The point is: Before you trust, you have to listen. But unless Christ's Word is preached, there's nothing to listen to."

Night after night, I had been lying in bed blanketed by the muggy July musk of Africa, lost in my thoughts and fears and expectations of what might happen based on what our lawyer said. During our days, we heard unfavorable speculations from the judge's office staff. We read sobering and sometimes heartbreaking articles and posts from others who'd been in our situation. But when Nate read the Bible aloud, we were grounded by a wholly different input. In his book *Psalms: The Prayer Book of the Bible*, Dietrich Bonhoeffer writes, "The richness of the Word of God ought to determine our prayer, not the poverty of our heart."[10] Nate and I both learned how deeply true it is that "the word of God is living and powerful" (Heb. 4:12). It is powerful enough to shift a heart, to change a situation, to shape our thoughts and perceptions. There is only one Truth, one source of input, that enables us to truly see beyond the limitations—and sometimes the lies—of our circumstances. And we can replace those limitations and lies with truth, spoken.

One minute at a time.

There are days when I circle the outside perimeter of our house in the early morning hours and speak the Psalms back to my heart, just as Nate circled our guest home all those years ago. Inside and fast asleep are the two little ones we brought home from that prayer-filled trip. I lift up their hurting hearts with words of truth, again and again.

As a family, we sometimes sing God's Word too. Though not all of us are singers, there's something about setting a passage of Scripture to a tune that allows those words to sink deep. Nearly every top-forty pop song that came out when I was a teenager has worked its way into my permanent memory bank. I'm at the grocery and find myself singing along with songs on the PA system that I haven't thought about for two decades. Music can sneak past our rational thinking and work its way into our operating system. This is why we sing God's

Word, even if we're off key. I not only want to remember these truths twenty years from now, I want them to become part of me. I want them to shape my thinking.

You can do this. Take a phrase from God's Word. Speak it aloud in the shower or as you pull out of the driveway for work. While in the carpool line or running errands, quiet the noise around you with the sound of your voice saying His Word. Win back your day one minute at a time with the truth of God's Word, or with a little ditty that sticks, and watch what happens to your heart as His truth begins to speak louder than all the other noise of the day. "Left to ourselves," writes pastor Eugene Peterson, "we will pray to some god who speaks what we like hearing, or to the part of God we manage to understand. But what is critical is that we speak to the God who speaks to us."[11]

Growth in God—reaching for Him and sinking our roots deep—doesn't happen passively. We have God's truth, and we can *wield* it. We can put it in our mouths and speak it, sing it, and declare it, because it is true.

Adore God.

If we sit sideways in the oversized leather chair, the one that was already faded and cracked before we got it, two of us can fit. Caleb's little body, tucked into last season's mismatched pajamas, presses beside mine as we all sit around the fire before the children go to bed, and I wonder just what might come out of this kid's mouth tonight.

He's still a mystery to me, this child. He was a toddler when we adopted him, and thus he has no memories of his life before becoming a Hagerty. He smiles and pops his collar like Nate and spends hours using his sisters' thread to string up plastic toys and Legos so he can hang them from the second-story banister. He's goofy and loud and all things boy, but some days the clouds hang low behind his eyes. They threaten to disrupt his young-boy lightfootedness. He has a history that one day will be fodder for his conversations with God, but right now he's not ready or able to talk.

I think my son is a mystery to himself too.

Those clouds of loss and grief hang low some days, and he can't wrap words around what feels so hard, so he grumbles. Something hurts. It's that dull ache again, but how does a young child process the kind of loss he faced before he even walked?

Each of my children processes their grief in different ways. One crawls into my lap, near weekly, and says, "I'm just having a hard, hard day." She makes the connections to her past without me. Her grief is tangible to her. Another cries in secret while I spend months readying myself for the small piece of her heart that she'll sanction for exploration when she's ready to talk.

But Caleb, he climbs trees and scouts for hawks and makes pets out of field mice, and one day he will discover that bravery is found in a bare heart. Until then, I wait with him. And we adore together. We take a phrase or sentence of God's Word that demonstrates who He is, and we tell it back to Him and to our own souls.

One evening, as Caleb's seven-year-old body sidled up to mine on the leather chair, we were adoring God based on Luke 2, the part when the heavenly host of angels announces God's joyous Christmas secret to poor shepherds.

"God, You didn't give Your secrets to just the wealthy or the kings," Caleb said. "You told them to people nobody cared about."

Caleb isn't yet old enough to verbalize his grief, to ask God questions about why his story has unfolded as it has. But he can recognize himself in the biblical story of others who lived a seemingly forgotten existence and yet were noticed by God. Through adoration, Caleb can try on a language about God that describes His love and His eye on the unnoticed. His words of adoration are leading his heart, making a way for him to process what he will one day feel and experience more directly. This is the crazy, transforming power of adoration. We use our words to praise God and in the process find ourselves getting healed of false perceptions of Him.

Caleb and I are teaching our souls to look up at God in wonder and awe, to give Him the praise He deserves and loves, even when we don't feel it. This is, perhaps, one of the most critical parts of adoration: *even when we don't feel it.*

In adoration, we take a phrase or sentence of God's Word, we see what those words say about who God is, and we speak them back to Him and to our own souls. We pattern our words toward praise in the midst of whatever we are feeling.

Our emotions can tell us a lot about how we see God, but if our emotions are left unfettered or unexamined, they can become a barrier to adoration. When we choose to practice adoration anyway in the midst of whatever we are feeling, our words lift us over that barrier and into a deeper connectedness with God. That's why we start our adoration right where we are—no platitudes or "Christianese" that paints a gloss over reality. We start from the grit of life, whether we're grumpy or overwhelmed, tired or angry. Adoration says, *Yes, my heart is just barely willing to praise, but that's okay. I'll start here.*

Adoration is a way to remind our souls who God is according to His Word. We take our eyes off of what we are not and where our circumstances are lacking and form words around His beauty and His truth. Adoration waters our friendship with God. He loves when we use our mouths to praise Him, and we train our hearts to look at Him, rather than what we're not, when we adore.

Recognize the truth about yourself in light of who God is.

A simple and gentle correction had sent my near-teenager into a downward spiral of shame right back to a dark part of her heart that questioned her worth and her value in God's eyes. And it wasn't the first time. Former orphans often wear what the rest of us get good at hiding. She's too young to have learned how to shove down shame, and Nate and I don't want her to. We want shame up and out, exposed before God and ready to be tended gently by His hands.

So on this night when she is once more cowering in shame, I have her stay up later than the other children. Together, we pull out sketchpads and colored pens and Scripture. Her inroad is art.

I open the Bible to the Psalms, to a verse that steadies me, rights me, when I feel most raw and ashamed: "He delivered me because He delighted in me" (Ps. 18:19).

She's writing it out, hand-lettering, and I'm praying, realizing as I pray how impossible it feels that an eleven-year-old girl with her history might understand God's delight. We'd all rather be workers, earners, than lovers of God. Working feels easier, more within reach, for the former orphan and for me.

As she carefully inks down the verse with her pen and I can tell her mind is wandering, I start to list out loud all the things I love about her, things I'm sure God loves about her too.

"Did you know that He loves when you dance in the kitchen and you think no one is looking? He loved the painting of the Blue Ridge Mountains you made for Daddy. He loves when you sing in the shower."

She's still sketching but also listening. I move on to "like," more akin to delight, yet harder for the achievement-seeking heart to understand.

"He likes when you play basketball in your rain boots. And that day when you tried out your bike in the snow, He really enjoyed you."

She cracks a smile, maybe starting to like this part of herself too, if God does.

"He likes that you read under the covers of your bed, late at night. He likes how neat you keep your drawers. He made you to love order."

"Mommy," she says, looking up at me, "am I the only person on the planet who has a hard time believing that God likes me?"

"Nope," I tell her. She's tapping into the deepest cry of the human heart, the heart that can preach a sermon on God's love one moment and flog itself in private over a single mistake the next. We all struggle to believe His delight. Might this be one of the greatest barriers to our communion with

God—believing that the one who made us barely likes us, the one we assume finds us barely tolerable?

I don't read Psalm 18:19 and immediately believe that God delights in me. But when I speak that verse back to Him—like my girl and I did that night as she sketched and I prayed after we talked—something inside me shifts a little more closely toward belief.

So much of the distance between God and us could be spanned if we'd let His Word inform us about who He is and who we are in Him. When we see God more clearly, we see ourselves more clearly.

My sweet daughter is learning to delight in what God loves and realizing a bit more every day that it is her.

They grumbled, critical. "For this fragrant oil might have been sold for much and given to the poor" (Matt. 26:9). They criticized Mary not only for what she did but for what she didn't do, and labeled her omission a moral failure.

This may have been the most sharply painful comment for her to hear, especially from ones she likely loved and trusted. Words that made her the most vulnerable, pained, if she caught herself caring more what others thought than what Jesus thought. Although her outpouring came from deep within her, it certainly would have been easier to offer it if no one else had known about it. Subjecting herself to the eyes of others in such a private moment was a sacrifice in itself.

Perhaps their comments echoed her own fears: *Should I*

have done something more worthwhile with this oil? Perhaps she second-guessed herself in a flash of insecurity. But she'd done it. She spilled a life savings over feet and floor. Gone. Done.

She might have noted scowls on their faces seconds before she poured the oil out, but it no longer mattered. She'd tasted the good thing. Again. She squandered the best of herself for love. And He received her as a friend.

She would be one who told others about Him. Who served. Who gave. But on that night, her service began with waste for God alone. And I like to think that in pouring herself out at His feet, she changed the world.

———————— *For Your Continued Pursuit* ————————

2 Chronicles 16:9 | Psalm 5:3 | Psalm 18:19 | Psalm 25:14 | Psalm 51:10 | Psalm 86:12 | Psalm 105:2 | Psalm 119:18 | Psalm 141:8 | Psalm 147 | Psalm 149:4 | Hosea 2:16 | Matthew 26:9 | Mark 1:35 | Luke 5:16 | John 6:63 | John 10:27 | John 10:30 | John 15:9 | John 15:15 | John 17:20 | Romans 10:17 | 2 Corinthians 4:18 | Ephesians 3:16–21 | Ephesians 5:18–20 | Colossians 3:16 | Hebrews 4:12–13 | Hebrews 5:7 | James 4:8 | Revelation 2:2–5

nine

VOICES

Hearing God's Truth above the Criticism and Chatter

"And they criticized her sharply."
—MARK 14:5

Several years ago on my birthday, we took the whole family out to dinner. With a young crew and a bank account freshly depleted from adoptions, a dinner out was no small thing. I felt my age this particular year but also felt a giddy anticipation akin to what most eight-year-olds might feel on their birthday. This meal was going to be good. The kids had been prepped that this evening was not about them. And I had curled my hair. I wasn't wearing sweatpants.

We arrived early for the dinner rush and were seated in a nearly empty restaurant. But the waitress assigned to our table was unhappy at hello. She rolled her eyes at our requests, muttered under her breath, and placed our drinks on the table as if she were a beleaguered official stamping passports. She didn't know this was my day to be celebrated. She didn't know I'd already fed my four children, twice, that day and bathed and dressed each one of them before getting there. We'd even clipped all sets of nails. *Toenails.*

Our waitress was too consumed by her own story to attend to mine. Our children's eyes were wide as they witnessed her undeniable irritation roiling around behind that drink tray. Between water refills, we whispered to the kids, "This is where we practice God's love."

They smiled big and called her ma'am and used an unusually high level of manners. Nate left her double his standard tip and told the children about it. It was easy for them—and for us—to love well that night because this waitress had no emotional hook in our hearts.

But what about when the emotional hook *is* there? Loving others who mistreat us is harder when our hearts are wrapped up tightly in the relationship, when the harsh words play directly to our fears, or when the mistreatment lasts for years and we're spinning in anger and hurt.

I've had both. The ache of someone I trust and look up to bruising my heart in their calloused hands, and the harsh words from one not as dear to me that played right into the center of my fears. I've faced waves of misunderstanding and judgment, often the kind that are especially hard to let go of. But I've also learned that hidden beneath those pounding waves is one of the best places to seek God.

How do You *see me, God?* isn't a question we consider asking when the world treats us as we feel we deserve.

Who am I from Your *perspective, God?* isn't a game-changing conversation when the relational mirrors around us make us feel good.

Jesus' instruction to turn the other cheek is all well and good until we're criticized or misunderstood and need to understand how God sees us in that moment.

When I've been wronged or unjustly criticized, I want to fight back. I want to grit my teeth and defend. Find justice. I want people in my circle to bend a sympathetic ear and to be on my side.

But when another human being doesn't see me clearly, I get to ask God who I am. When I'm on the receiving end of judgment or mistreatment, I get to carve a space in my prayer closet where only one voice matters. When rough hands hurt what is tender within me, I get to scoot up next to the one whose hands formed me.

And so, in some ways, the one who mistreats me gives me a gift: the gift of collapsing into the arms of God. What happens in the secret place between God and me is out of that person's reach, making it even sweeter.

Sometimes when I'm under God's kind eyes, I see that my opponent isn't all that wrong. And I'm not all that right. Other times, I still feel wounded and misunderstood. The real battle here isn't for a winner, for me over the other person, but to win over new places of my heart to God's gentle perspective on me.

When we believe that a life poured out for God is our most beautiful expression, every accusation and misunderstanding carries within it an opportunity to step into that beauty, just in a way we might not have chosen.

If we can find a place to pause from the swirl, the answer becomes clear: the ones who oppose us when we need championing the most are also the ones who send us into the hidden conversations with God, conversations that change us. God champions us like no human can, but we don't often see that unless we have nowhere to look but Him.

I can allow those who misjudge me to help me become more of a daughter, one who comes to her Daddy in a whole new needy way when she's been mistreated. I can bless those who curse me because of how He whispers to me when I'm mistreated. In the light of Him who loves me, I can face my fear of not being loved. Thomas Merton says it this way: "If we are to love sincerely and with simplicity, we must first of all overcome the fear of not being loved."[12]

Why wouldn't I give them—the critics, the judgers, the misunderstanders—my other cheek, my favorite coat, my tired extra mile?

"Blessed are you when they revile and persecute you, and say all kinds of evil against you falsely for My sake," says Jesus in the Sermon on the Mount. "Rejoice and be exceedingly glad, for great is your reward in heaven, for so they persecuted the prophets who were before you" (Matt. 5:11–12).

We read these words and yet too often still experience surprise when our best efforts at Christian living result in something other than Christian applauding. *Do the works of God and people will see and they will celebrate,* we think. We forget that the map for following God was given to us by a man who was routinely persecuted by the religious leaders of

His day, who was abandoned by virtually all of His followers at the end of His life and then brutally murdered.

We want our work to be known and our impact to be memorialized. And it will be, but by God alone. No human can give us accolades that will satisfy the deepest longings of our hearts. We search vainly from others for the acclaim that only God can give.

This is why we need to reframe the way we view and respond to mistreatment. If we can see it as a form of hiding in God, it takes on new significance. In God's hands, it becomes a tool He uses to redirect the human heart toward finding its value in Him rather than in other human beings. When we learn to relish what happens in the hidden place, we lean into what He wants to offer us in mistreatment.

We all face routine human misunderstandings and relational challenges, the scuffles that happen as our lives brush up against another. Your best gift today may be the one who misunderstands you or even opposes you. Your adversary may actually be your advocate, the one moving you closer to God.

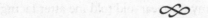

What did Mary think others would say about her when she undid her hair and wasted her inheritance on Jesus' feet? Perhaps she had to overcome days of fear, knowing that she was about to do something unwelcome and strange. Perhaps she was so focused on adoring Him that she never considered what other voices would say. Perhaps her thoughts of doubt were her biggest enemy. Or what if her action wasn't planned at all? What if her impulsive rush of devotion overshadowed even the thought of onlookers' opinions?

Mary had already unfurled her heart before this Savior along the dusty road, talking with Him after the crowds went home. She'd developed a history with this man in the private spaces of her heart and in the private pockets of her day. His voice had become bigger to her than any other voice, any other noise.

But the criticism that night was sharp. Biting. These were not strangers. They were people she knew well. People whose opinions she valued. Out of the weakest parts of themselves, they spoke words that lodged in the weakest parts of her. They knew how to hurt. They knew how to play on the criticisms she likely already told herself.

But Mary had developed the habit of valuing Jesus' voice above all others.

She knew she'd come for Him alone.

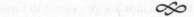

"I just can't hear God," my ten-year-old told me after facing her sin. She'd participated in an unfettered rant toward her siblings and was having a hard time turning her heart and repenting. She was simply mad, and the suggestion I'd made for her to quiet herself for a few minutes and talk to God only positioned her to field more of her desperate anger. She was both defensive and defeated, not wanting to admit fault yet feeling irrevocably flawed and stuck on the inside. I guess this line of thinking isn't age discriminate. This young one was discovering that sometimes accusations and criticisms come not just from outside voices but also from voices on the inside. When the accusation is internal, we can't merely acknowledge it and move on. We need to challenge it by putting up a fight.

My daughter's thoughts had been brewing for hours after a morning altercation in the kitchen with her sister over a skillet of eggs. I could see in her eyes that her dark thoughts had taken over. She'd become their slave, responding to what ricocheted around her mind. No wonder she'd had difficulty with a simple request to set the dinner table.

And she couldn't understand His offer of kindness for her repentance, gently inviting her to turn. This incident only proved to her what she'd already felt on the inside: she was wrong. Just bad.

Trying to think quickly, I pulled out a notebook and began sketching. I drew an outline of her head, leaving the space within empty, void of the voice of God just as she described it and just as she felt it, though I knew her mind was full of other voices.

"Tell me exactly what thoughts have gone through your mind this afternoon," I said. "Let's take a closer look at what's inside of there."

After some coaxing, we made a list. On it were statements like, "I'm a bad person," and, "I'm not a good sister," and, "I keep messing up." For every thought she mentioned, I made a hash mark across the head of this rough sketch. When we were finished, there was no white space left. No room in her mind for anything but her own accusing thoughts.

"Now, where's the room to hear God?" I asked, holding up the notebook.

She smiled, coyly.

"I get it, baby girl," I said to her as I scooted up close to her. "I'm almost thirty years older than you, and in one single day I can lose all the white space in my head too. My mind can get full of all sorts of things that keep me from hearing God."

Maybe you can relate.

She is just beginning to learn what I still need to practice to stay alive in God: every single thought matters. The thoughts that don't bow to God will give permission to another god. But a barreling life leaves little room for evaluating these unfettered thoughts. It leaves little room for letting God's rest and His peace seep in and His truth invade the cacophony in my mind.

Responding to the clock and reacting to our to-do lists and chasing the latest thrill in front of us—yes, even the good-work-of-His-kingdom kind of thrill—keeps the mind that's not at peace in motion. The quick decision to forfeit quiet to read another's status update keeps our minds racing, with no space to consider which thoughts of ours are aligning with God and His Word. Just like my daughter hears *I keep messing up*, we let the noise take charge of the uncertain parts of us, often without even knowing it.

The white space of the day is God's gift to us. Discovering the white space of our minds on which He can write is what we're invited to find, there. The hum of the washing machine as we fold our load from the dryer. The still of two o'clock in the afternoon before the bus unloads children and backpacks and giggles. The sigh of a prayer as we sit down to a good meal. All of these moments remind us, by comparison, of the noise that happens within our minds the rest of the time.

It's one thing to get rid of the noise. It's another thing to know how to invite Him into the white space.

It's Tuesday afternoon.

The babe's down for his nap, the children are building forts in the backyard woods, and Nate is working from home with one eye on the computer while answering to shouts of "Daddy, we found a turtle. Come see!" and "Is it time for a snack yet?" and "Can we ride bikes down the hill?" The baby monitor drones in the background at home as I get in the car to drive a few miles to a coffee shop. Tuesday afternoons are my time to write.

As I pull away from the house, my thoughts go something like this: First, I remember all the things I've left undone at home. *Is the oven on? I forgot to check Lily's reading. Ooh, the bread for dinner is still in the freezer.*

If unchecked, that line of thinking can escalate from a simple question, *Should I just turn around?* to questioning my worth and my calling: *What I am thinking, trying to add writing to my life? Who do I think I am?* By the time I walk through the door of the coffee shop, order a chai, and sit down, I'm in a slump, less enthusiastic about my writing now that I've reminded myself of all that I "should" be doing and all the ways I'm unqualified to do anything at all.

Then I glance at the young woman two tables over, writing away on her computer. A school paper, maybe, or a book? She looks intent. Having entered my rut of unfettered thoughts, I'm susceptible to more: *The world doesn't need another writer. There are so many people saying something, anything. Why do I want to add my voice to that noise?* The writing idea that had been bumping around in my mind for days suddenly seems foolish. I cross a line through it on my page of handwritten notes.

I'm better off just getting lost in a book today, I reason, and so I join the throngs of writers and painters and accountants and schoolteachers and photographers who forfeit God's display of glory through them in exchange for a lie.

I join the mothers who kiss their children goodnight, only to walk back into the kitchen in shame at the tone they'd used five minutes earlier. *I knew I'd never be a good mother.* The painters who get their equipment together for an afternoon of playing with God only to end the day with an empty canvas. *If I can't get it just right, I'm not ready to try.* The bankers and lawyers and architects who spend every commute berating themselves for not hitting the achievement marks they think they should. *I'm just an unqualified faker underneath this suit.*

The accusations in my head and yours aren't just personal report cards. They are arrows from an enemy who is hounding our lives and our pursuit of God. "For we do not wrestle against flesh and blood" (Eph. 6:12). The enemy is exploiting our weak spots, the ones that have the potential to bring the greatest glory of God into our lives, and we've been duped. The enemy is, after all, a destroyer of what is good. When we let shameful lies speak louder than vulnerable expressions of our true selves, we are missing a meeting with God. When we hear Satan's lies and respond with an acceptance letter, God is still inviting us: *Engage with Me in the place where you feel less-than or ashamed. I'll breathe My truth over your dark thoughts.*

When we hear the cacophony of accusing voices on the inside of us, we don't have to surrender to them. We fight those lies with spoken truth: "For we do not wrestle against flesh and blood." We recognize that God made us to fight the battle against our untruthful thoughts: "Therefore take up the whole armor of God, that you may be able to withstand in the evil day, and having done all, to stand" (v. 13).

In the hidden places, we realize that the Word of God is a powerful weapon, not something created just for a cross-stitched wall hanging or as generally helpful advice. It reaches into our insides, into our inner thoughts and intentions, and exposes us before the God who has made us to partner with Him and against the internal lies we battle. "For the word of God is living and powerful, and sharper than any two-edged sword, piercing even to the division of soul and spirit, and of joints and marrow, and is a discerner of the thoughts and intents of the heart. And there is no creature hidden from His sight, but all things are naked and open to the eyes of Him to whom we must give account" (Heb. 4:12–13).

So how do we battle these accusing voices? Start by jotting down the self-defeating thoughts you entertain, the ones with which you often agree. Thoughts like, *I'm never going to change*, as you look at parts of yourself that long have been sedentary and unbending. *I'm not worth sticking with*, after a vulnerable moment with a friend. *I'm just setting myself up for another big failure*, when stepping out into something new. These thoughts will dictate your emotions and your actions if you let them. These are the enemy's accusations and lies. When they creep in and you see them for what they truly are, renounce them with God's truth. Refuse to agree with them. Fill your mouth with life, recognizing that "death and life are in the power of the tongue" (Prov. 18:21). Power is in speaking what is true.

Instead of saying to yourself, *I'm never going to change*, renounce the lie that a heart is forever unbending. Repent for agreeing with these thoughts that do not line up with God's Word. Lean into God's power to work in you, even though your fears speak otherwise. As you pray for yourself, repeat back to God, "He who began a good work in [me] will carry it on to completion until the day of Christ Jesus" (Phil. 1:6 NIV).

Instead of, *I'm not worth sticking with*, renounce the lie that you are unlovable and unworthy. Repent of agreeing with this lie and ask God to hear the cries of your heart to have a friend who knows you in your pain. Use the words of the psalmist: "In the day when I cried out, You answered me, and made me bold with strength in my soul" (Ps. 138:3). The Word of God equips you to fight back when you hear those toxic mutterings.

Instead of, *I'm just setting myself up for a big failure*, renounce the lie that the worst is yet to come. Repent of disregarding the hope of Jesus for your life and agreeing with hopeless expectations. Ask God to awaken your life in prayer and to show you, afresh, how He hears you. Use the words of the psalmist:

Many are they who say of me,
"There is no help for him in God."

But You, O LORD, are a shield for me,
My glory and the One who lifts up my head.
I cried to the LORD with my voice,
And He heard me from His holy hill.

—PSALM 3:2–4

In His Word, we have help, especially for the lies many of us have just accepted as part of life. I often find the help I need in the Psalms, which is sometimes called the prayer book of the Bible. The Psalms includes prayers that run the gamut of human experience from prayers of thanksgiving and praise to prayers of lament and confession. God gives us these prayers not only to help us express our thoughts and emotions to Him but also to help us hear His truth above the world's chatter. Author and pastor Tim Keller says of the Psalms, "We are not simply to read the Psalms; we are to be immersed in them so that they profoundly shape how we relate to God . . . [They] are the divinely ordained way to learn devotion to our God."[13] The Psalms demonstrates that we can bring to God all of ourselves—with all of our emotions—and trust that He has the power to change us.

When I feel helpless and hopeless and alone, I pray, "My soul clings to the dust; revive me according to Your word" (Ps. 119:25).

When I've messed up big, I pray, "Purge me with hyssop, and I shall be clean; wash me, and I shall be whiter than snow" (Ps. 51:7).

When I'm filled with anxiety, I pray, "In the day when I cried out, You answered me, and made me bold with strength in my soul" (Ps. 138:3).

And when I start to feel worthless, unnoticed, and over-looked, I pray, "Keep me as the apple of Your eye; hide me under the shadow of Your wings" (Ps. 17:8).

I pray when I feel helpless and hopeless and alone. I choose with my words to lay myself bare before Him instead of standing at a distance from Him and chastising myself for how I've fallen short. My emotions—the ones that a full schedule and an outwardly productive life can help prevent me from feeling—are a road to conversation with God. The hidden places of my heart get exposed and He responds.

When we let the Psalms or any biblical truth sink into the white spaces in our lives and minds, we are winning one of the most significant battles of our lives. We learn to lean into Him for a win. Just as it was with my daughter, our minds are often full of myriad unfettered thoughts, such that there is little room to receive God's thoughts. When these words go beyond falling lightly within our hearing, when we allow them to sink deeply into us—reading, memorizing, speaking, singing, and praying them—we find that our white space expands. "[The Psalms] are written to be prayed, recited, and sung," Keller writes, "to be done, not merely to be read."[14] We work less to crowd out the noise in our minds and realize that the white spaces aren't the empty times of our day or vacant parts of our minds waiting to be stuffed. They are pregnant, full in themselves. And expansive.

At the break of day, noon, night, and a dozen times in

between, God's Word is your ally. Read it. Say it. Sing it. To live and thrive in God amid all the competing noise and voices of this age, we have to engage with His Word. Not just once a day or once every few days. We can't live without this Word.

So we lean into God, in hiding. We lean into Him in the late afternoon when we see the sun illuminate the dust on our coffee tables, speaking the Word of God against the lies that have been infecting our day. We lean into Him on the Saturday without any plans, asking Him to speak into the void and remind us that there is no void in God.

The Word of God is powerful against our internal traffic. It pierces through our souls, even to the parts of us we've hidden from ourselves. It reaches into our spirits with His Spirit, breathing life as He moves in. It replaces the internal chatter of life—the criticisms, the comparisons, and the shoulds—with the truth of what God sees and thinks and feels. And that's a beautiful sound.

It's just after dusk and the children are in bed. I can hear the clock that's been ticking, unnoticed, all day. I can hear the quiet.

I have much I could be doing. But I also have an invitation: *Let yourself hear My voice. Express your emotions through the Psalms. Be silent with Me. Let go of the voices, the noise, the chatter.*

I don't write a blog post about the exchange. I don't snap a picture. Only God and I know the details of our conversation. And an hour later, the only evidence that it was time well spent is hidden underneath my skin. My heart grew. He loved my private reach at an unplanned time. He responded. He loved the opportunity to marvel at His own craftsmanship in me.

It's time for bed on a Tuesday and I have nothing to show for it.

Tonight has been wildly successful.

———————— *For Your Continued Pursuit* ————————

Psalm 17:8 | Psalm 51:7 | Psalm 119:25 | Psalm 138:3 | Proverbs 18:21 | Song of Songs 2:14 | Isaiah 26:3 | Zechariah 3:1–5 | Matthew 5:11–12 | Matthew 5:39 | Mark 14:3–9 | John 10:10 | Romans 2:4 | 2 Corinthians 10:4–6 | Ephesians 6:10–20 | Philippians 1:6 | Philippians 4:8 | Hebrews 4:11–13 | 1 Peter 2:21–25 | 1 Peter 4:12–14

ten

THIRSTY SEASONS

Learning to Long for God's Presence

"Me you do not have always."

—MARK 14:7

We were warned before adopting our kids that adoption might ruin us. If you walked into my kitchen at 5:00 p.m. the first winter after one of our adoptions, you might have indeed thought we were ruined. I surely did, then.

The sun sank earlier every day, and my daughter sank right with it. The cause changed daily. Not enough food at dinner, too many crumbs to sweep from the kitchen floor, and a sibling's accidental elbow bump all made her wail. Night after night we fielded the sobs, knowing it was easier for her to cry over spilled milk than to go into the crux of her pain, loss that no five-year-old should ever have to face.

So we held her in the tears and wondered if we'd ever know normal again. As I ushered children into their jammies each evening, I prayed a new kind of prayer—short and desperate. I was tired and needy and confused. I had no book to tell me what to expect from a child with her history, her particular cocktail of losses and grief. Even the best parenting strategies were not sufficient. I needed God.

Our family struggled so much during this time that, yes, some might have said we were truly ruined. But a change was taking place inside me that had started years before and is still working its way through me. Instead of running from my weaknesses, I started to lean into them.

I began to like the benefits of unraveling my heart at the feet of Jesus, who never promised I would have strength of my own. I studied His expression toward me when I brought nothing but tears to our conversation. He promises in His Word to care for the brokenhearted. I began to realize that the brokenhearted weren't the ones I pitied from my cushioned life. They were me. I was brokenhearted.

My children didn't ruin me. I was ruined long before they came along. However, my children did bring me into circumstances that God used to show me how weak I really am. Terribly weak, it turns out. I am no more ruined now than I was when life ran on time, the laundry was always immediately folded, and I knew what to expect out of each day. It's just that now I can see my ruination more clearly. I can see how much I need God.

Out of my weakness, and yours, can come a glorious thirst for God. What some may call the end of us, the ruin of us, can bring us closer to God than any one of our strongest days. We think, *When I get there [to that elusively strong place], then I'll rest, be satisfied, be confident, change the world, [fill in the blank].* And then we go to embarrassing lengths to claw our way out of any situation that leaves us feeling helpless. We do anything to feel strong again, even if that strength is a shadow. But God's invitation to us is and always will be, *Die to this illusion of strength you've created. That's when you'll find what you've been thirsting for.* God created us to want more of Him. He created us to thirst for Him. He created us to need Him, even when all we want to need is ourselves.

Today, Hope pirouettes through the kitchen and Caleb stores books under chairs so he can read them between chores and Lily paints us a picture of a boat for our bedroom that's better than anything I've ever bought from a store. Eden belts out hymns in the shower and Bo is learning to snuggle close and pat my hand when I'm sick. I love these banner moments when my children are happy and enjoying life. But these best moments with my children are not what truly bring out the best in me. It's in all those not-shining moments that these beautiful children have made me want to rest on God's chest, that place where I've crumbled and where He moved in with power. I'm weepy and He's gentle. I'm burdened and He's kind.

I'm reaching. Thirsty. And He responds.

The degree to which I allow weakness to become thirst for more of God, and the degree to which I allow myself to lean into that thirst rather than run from it, is the degree to which I am becoming my best self.

It's a verse you've likely seen in a church foyer or cross-stitched on your grandmother's wall: "As the deer pants for the water brooks, so pants my soul for You, O God" (Ps. 42:1). Perhaps it was written in calligraphy beneath an image of a majestic deer quietly drinking from a sun-dappled stream. It's an idyllic, peaceful scene. But what if the psalmist had a different scene in mind? What if the deer had a desperate thirst? A deer that *pants* for water might be running from death, nearly frantic for water.

Maybe you've experienced a version of that desperate physical thirst. Perhaps you were in intense heat and without any water for hours or miles. It's a terribly uncomfortable condition to be in. It's also incredibly vulnerable. When you're dehydrated and thirsty, thirst is all consuming.

What if this desperate thirst is the scene the psalmist had in mind? A soul full of such longing for God that nothing else matters. And a thirst that is actually a good thing, an indicator of present and coming growth.

Though it seems counterintuitive, the spaces in our lives where God seems to be absent are sometimes the places where we grow the most. If we can tolerate the thirst long enough, staying in our weakness and our need, we will find more of God.

Every few years, I circle back to the same reminder, the same invitation. Each time, it's with a little more clarity and a growing readiness to lean into Him in my weakness.

Just after I birthed our first biological child, who was the fifth child in our family, I remembered that familiar feeling returning, the one where I felt I was sinking while those around me remained afloat. My "bigs" had growing heart-needs alongside their growing bodies, and yet there was only one me, one mommy, for all of them. Now I had *five* of them. I found myself making a daily mental record of their needs and my gaps, allowing a steady drip of self-resentment about my human weakness to leak into my thinking. I was tempted to despise this season in which I felt mostly weak and incapable.

But God reminded me to allow for the thirst. I heard Him while I nursed the babe and between all the heart-needs that surfaced in a day. I heard Him when I slowed down to evaluate, and not just imbibe, my thoughts and fears. This was an invitation: to lean. In.

It took hidden times, desperate times, for me to practice leaning into my weaknesses rather than despising them. Whereas I once responded to experiences of weakness by adding another spiritual discipline or seeking a new ministry opportunity or chiding myself for my discomforting thirst, now I was praying prayers like this:

I want more of You, God.
Grow me, on the inside.
I'm thirsty. Fill me, God.

I could have slaked my thirst with temporary fixes. Every day was filled with dozens of distractions that tried to woo my attention away from this uncomfortable void inside me. I was a God-follower who did not and could not *feel* God, and all I wanted was not to feel that way any more—not to be so vulnerable and parched. *What is wrong with me?* But I kept seeing thirst come up in His Word:

- "You, God, are my God, earnestly I seek you; I thirst for you, my whole being longs for you, in a dry and parched land where there is no water" (Ps. 63:1 NIV).
- "I spread out my hands to you; I thirst for you like a parched land" (Ps. 143:6 NIV).

- "Blessed are those who hunger and thirst for righteousness, for they shall be filled" (Matt. 5:6).
- "Ho! Everyone who thirsts, come to the waters; and you who have no money, come, buy and eat. Yes, come, buy wine and milk without money and without price" (Isa. 55:1).

"Feel the gap and fill it" had been my approach to life in God up to that point. But now I was in a desperate situation, and I needed freedom to say, "I'm empty. It's okay to be empty and stay empty for a little while." That admission led to this prayer: *I really do want more of You, God. I want more than what I am experiencing and knowing right now.* And I let myself feel the dryness of thirst without trying to fix it on my own.

Realizing that my thirst wasn't wrong but could instead increase my reach for God surfaced an eagerness in me. I read His Word and prayed with greater expectation. I waited with eyes open. I noticed Him in places I hadn't seen Him before and in ways I hadn't allowed Him to come to me before.

In the early years after our adoption, I was alarmed when my children's deep wounds manifested themselves in some way. I felt both ill-equipped to respond and skittish about what might lie ahead—for them and for me. Their weakness made me acutely aware of my own. I wanted to crawl out of my skin, here. I certainly didn't feel a staying power as I faced these chasms in myself.

"Do something, *anything*, God, to change this. To change them," I'd pray, desperate not to feel so vulnerable. Desperate to stop the pain in them and in me. But God used this desperation to intensify a thirst in my soul. A thirst I didn't have when my children and our home felt normal, when I didn't feel so exposed. A thirst that offered an opportunity to reach. To lean in. To stay in that place of internal floundering want.

In a culture that's full—full of commitments, full of tasks, full of opportunities and people and digital windows into lives that aren't our own—God calls us to resist succumbing to readily available distractions and instead to press into these thirsty moments, our weakest seasons. Thirst is our ally. We want to be thirsty for God.

This is a beautiful paradox of the spiritual life. Jesus invites us to come to Him and then makes this promise: "But whoever drinks the water I give them will never thirst. Indeed, the water I give them will become in them a spring of water welling up to eternal life" (John 4:14 NIV).

Yet there remains this conundrum: we still feel parched for Him.

Before heaven, before completeness, before the end of lack, we can rest in our thirst, in this longing for God. When our thirst for more of God deepens our awareness of how much we need Him, our capacity for Him grows. We not only see Him as the spring of water, but we develop a continued and ever-growing thirst for *that* water. Our thirst is how God allures us. The thirsty don't just find God, they *thrive* in God. They drink with deep satisfaction. And this drink makes them thirsty for all that will one day be.

∞

"Me you do not have always."

Jesus had just acknowledged His impending death. In polite company and over dinner. He often upended social mores.

He spoke not to Mary but to the dinner guests who'd criticized her. Yet it was within her hearing. And on this night of her outpouring. Here, in one of her most vulnerable moments, Jesus made it clear He was not long for this earth.

Perhaps His statement shocked her. Or maybe it simply confirmed the sad truth she already suspected. She would know His face, His smile, that look He often gave her just a little longer. Then she would know the sharp pain of His absence, sharper still because she had stared into that face. It was her love for Him that made the longing for Him so great. The memories she had with this God-man as she sat at His feet would fuel an ache for her reunion with Him that would never quite subside until it happened.

Mary was made to move from thirst to fulfillment to thirst again, only to look toward a forever fulfillment one day still to come. Thirst and being satisfied in God would be interwoven for the rest of her days.

These were her growth spurts in God.

And this night, though thirst would come again, she found herself overflowing as she emptied her love at Jesus' feet.

Bo has six teeth, and only Nate gets a full toothy reveal.

All seven of us were around the dinner table laughing at

the antics of our one-year-old. Deep belly laughs and a single one-syllable word (at varying decibels) to describe just about everything. For his siblings, this babe is better entertainment than an electric train. And at the dinner table, Daddy draws out the best of that kid.

So there he was, the spitting image of his father and sitting four seats away, showing off all those teeth in one direction.

"I saw your baby pictures, Daddy, and he looks just like you," said Hope casually between bites.

"His hair is turning out to be the same color as yours, and his eyes are blue too," says Eden. "You know, Daddy, I think he looks just like you."

"Nah," says Nate. "We'll have to just wait and see what he looks like." In other conversations like this, he's reminded Caleb how many people say he and Caleb look alike but for the color of their skin. I do the same thing. Partially out of habit and partially to pacify the terrible ache of their loss.

As the girls move on to talking about hair color, Nate jumps in: "Your hair color is the same brown as Mommy's." They disagree. Mine's lighter, they argue.

Everyone is taking bites and weighing in on hair color and eyes and the varying skin tones of one another (a common discussion in our home). I join the conversation with uneasy laughter, and yet this moment, for me, feels supercharged.

Nate and I want each of our kids to know and experience the God whose face is set fiercely toward them. This is the God who wants to heal their hearts, the hearts that may soon ache over the blank pages of their baby books—the ones unnaturally at the beginning. When that day comes, we want them to know they can cry at His feet. They can pour out the grief they feel when they realize that they may never see on earth the faces of the beautiful women who birthed them.

When the pain makes them want to pretend all that loss never happened, we want our children to feel the hands of God as He cups their chins and looks into their eyes with limitless understanding of their pain. We want them to have a tender brush with the God who came to not just reset the bones of their brokenness but make their broken hearts sing. But for that to happen, we have to let them feel the hurt, to feel the longing for something more. If we insulate them instead or somehow teach them to avoid the ache and the thirst of their history, we're giving them permission to overlook the most enrapturing parts of their God.

The same applies to you and me. If I constantly try to avoid how spiritually parched I feel, I'm missing the infilling nature of God, the one who doesn't just acknowledge my desert but gives me a stream, right there. Laughter is an incredible gift, and we as a family grab it when we can. It is healing. Yet if Nate or I or any one of these beloved children around our table refuses to look at and grieve our losses, we may also miss our most profound story in God.

As long as we're on earth, we *will* thirst for God. And He will respond. It may not be in the way we expect or within our timing, but He promises to respond to the thirsty. It's His way with us. Not just intellectually assenting to this but being willing to live in it, with Him, is what releases us from resenting the places that reveal how thirsty we are.

My children's wounds and needs remind me how much I need God. *I'm thirsty for more than a quick fix.*

An unexpected afternoon alone makes me feel barren in a way that I didn't notice the day before in a packed schedule. *I notice now that I need Him. I'm thirsty for Him to come and meet me.*

Being an indistinct face in a large crowd makes me want to be seen. *I'm thirsty for acknowledgment of the little movements of my life. But I'm really thirsty for His eyes, on me.*

I can welcome thirst when it prompts me to reach for God in the driest places.

Tenderly.

"I will lead her into the desert and speak tenderly to her there" (Hos. 2:14 NLT). These are God's words about His wayward people, spoken to the prophet Hosea, who had a wayward wife named Gomer. God's plan required a desert—an arid, dusty, inhospitable climate. Today, our desert equivalent could be our corners of hiddenness. Our anonymous cubicles. Our support roles. Our 3:00 a.m. baby feedings. Our fifteenth sojourn in the doctor's waiting room with an ill child, condition still undiagnosed. Our 136th day in the carpool line. Our crowded church sanctuaries. Our Friday nights alone. Our monotonous shifts in the grocery store that barely pay the bills.

It is there, in whatever this desert is, that He promises to speak tenderly.

What feels like a wilderness, a desert—the hidden seasons

and the hidden spaces throughout our day that expose how dry we are on the inside—cannot thwart the maker of rain. These are the times our roots forge deeper through the earth to find the water source. It's the only way to survive drought.

> For I will pour water on the thirsty land,
> and streams on the dry ground;
> I will pour out my Spirit on your offspring,
> and my blessing on your descendants.
> They will spring up like grass in a meadow,
> like poplar trees by flowing streams.

> —Isaiah 44:3–4 NIV

Our water is Him. This beautiful God. His eyes, they know us—all the parts of us. His arms, they're strong and they hold us. His whisper speaks life and breathes dust off what's old and needs reviving.

We drink of Him—this living water—and we want to drink again. It's that good. This God-man is *that* surprisingly good, better than any other single thing with which we've tried to slake our thirst. We're not trapped in these parched and hidden moments where no one sees us; instead, we're invited to sink our roots deeper into God right there. To stay long enough to hear God's tender voice over that specific moment, for us.

Thirst makes us reach for God not just as *the* Healer but as *our* Healer. And we watch the water pour on desert lands.

——————— *For Your Continued Pursuit* ———————

Psalm 33:16–22 | Psalm 34:18 | Psalm 42 | Psalm 63:1–8 | Psalm 81:10 | Psalm 84:1–4, 10 | Psalm 119:20, 81 | Psalm 143:6 | Psalm 147:3, 10–11 | Proverbs 27:7 | Isaiah 41:18–20 | Isaiah 44:3–4 | Isaiah 55:1 | Isaiah 61:1–3 | Hosea 2:14 | Matthew 5:6 | Matthew 9:15 | Mark 14:7 | John 4:1–26 | John 6:33–35 | John 7:37 | 2 Corinthians 12:8–10 | Ephesians 3:19 | 2 Timothy 2:13

eleven

GOD IS FOR US

Healing in the Hiding

"She has done what she could."
—MARK 14:8

M ommy, I think God wants me to tell you why I don't like Ethiopia," my five-year-old told me, so matter-of-fact.

I'd been waiting for this day. It just came about five years earlier than I'd anticipated. Over the course of the few years since she'd come home, any mention of Ethiopia left my little girl eyes-to-the-floor.

"We love Ethiopia!" I once declared to an Ethiopian coffee-shop barista as I slid a sleeve over my cup of tea. She had noticed my kids, recognized something familiar in their faces, and they had noticed her. But as we walked away, my little one said under her breath, "I don't love Ethiopia."

As her language skills and cognitive development advanced, I asked questions, trying to understand her disdain, but to no avail. We prayed in private, Nate and I, knowing that the secrets her little body held would become toxic if not brought into the light.

It wasn't until all four of us were in Uganda chasing papers for our two other daughters that I sensed God's prompting: *Now. She's ready to talk now.*

It happened to be the day we'd set aside for a mommy-daughter date during those waiting days after finally meeting the two older girls. I held my little one's hand as we walked on the dusty road from our guesthouse to the nearest spot for a cup of tea. She rambled about anything that came to mind, excited to have Mommy all to herself.

As she sat sipping her milk from a straw, she cracked open what she called her prayer journal to a picture she had drawn of a brown hut. She remembered. I wasn't sure that she would.

The minutes that followed felt like years as I listened to my little girl speak about big girl things—things I'd never taught her, things she saw in real life, not on a television or movie screen. It was as if she had grown up in one morning, suddenly able to articulate her pain, loss, and disappointment—and all the scenes that brought them about—with a coherence that didn't fit her age.

I choked back tears, just listening. I was stunned equally by her vivid account and her ability to communicate it. So many pieces of her puzzle came together in that one conversation. Gaps in our understanding of her suddenly filled.

When she was through, we talked. We prayed to ask Jesus to reveal how He felt about her and how He saw her during those lonely years.

I sat there praying: *What do I do now with these shards of glass, the remnants of her pain?* Then I saw the answer on her face. It went something like this: *Now I've told you everything,*

Mommy, so what are we having for lunch? It was finished, at least for now—wrapped up, handed to Mommy for safekeeping, and finally off five-year-old shoulders never meant to carry such a burden.

Since that conversation, her steps have been lighter. After that point, in her pretend play, she was often a transcontinental traveler, Ethiopia being one of her main stops. "I want to go back to Ethiopia one day and tell them about Jesus," she said to me recently.

God took this part of her burden. "He heals the brokenhearted and binds up their wounds" (Ps. 147:3). My little girl was climbing her way out, early, of brokenness. She was remembering, and acknowledging, the pain—the pain that creates space and emptiness and looks to God for healing.

This is, too, what the process of climbing out of brokenness looks like for me some days. A friend says something that stings, and instead of mentally rolling my eyes at her or looking for ways to defame her in my thinking, I ask God, *Why does this hurt?* I turn my attention away from my friend and toward God. I ask Him about me: *What is it in me that You want to heal? What is it in me that needs Your touch because these words hurt?*

As I lift my hurts, big and small, to God, I've often been surprised by how God shows up to heal everything. Even the parts of me I thought were unfixable, sedentary, "just part of my personality," or "just part of my story."

So many little aches or obstinate quirks that we accept about ourselves are places in our lives that God can heal, into which He can breathe His perspective. But for Him to

speak a healing word over old wounds, we have to acknowledge them.

My girl started young. He led her there. This was the first
of many conversations just like it she will have with Him in
the years ahead.

He loves to heal what has broken.

One Sunday after church, I was talking to new friends—new
to me, to us, and to our story. I knew that when they looked
at our family on Sundays, they saw colorful headbands and
cute boots on this one day of the week when we all looked
fairly well kempt. They saw rescue and redemption in the
intermingled line-up of light and dark skin, and they saw
my babes taking turns being lifted into Nate's arms during
worship. But I saw what they couldn't. I knew what simmered
beneath the patterned dresses and pressed shirts. I had held
those same babes the night before when one complained of
the nightmares again and the other cried for no identifiable
reason—and for every reason.

One of my girls sidled up beside me in this conversation
with new friends. She was brewing with pain from the
day before but dressed as if the American dream was hers.
When my new friends asked her a few questions, she looked
down and then away. She mumbled something under the
hand she uses to hide herself when she is shaky and unsure.
She was weary, and this invitation to chat with smiley
strangers only exacerbated her fatigue. But if you didn't

know her history, you might have written her off as a rude preadolescent.

A few minutes later, the conversation was over and we were putting on gloves and coats and walking to the parking lot. I slid into the car, embarrassed and sulking.

My daughter hadn't "performed."

In just a three-minute conversation, I felt trapped by imagined judgment from people I barely knew.

How do I get her to stop this? I grumbled about my apparently sullen child. *What if she still can't look someone in the eye when she's thirty? How can I ever take her anywhere if she continues to do this?*

That morning, I felt like I'd failed to live up to the image of a stellar parent who was facilitating redemption in her child's heart. Instead, I looked like I was aiding and abetting disrespectful children, clearly indulging self-centeredness by not addressing it on the spot.

Three minutes after a three-minute conversation and I was sunk. I perceived another's perspective and received it as truth—for my daughter and for me.

On the drive home, I took deep breaths and felt even worse about what was bubbling out of my heart than about what had actually happened. Hours later, I finally sat myself before God, asking Him to bring wisdom and healing to these hidden parts of me.

My response to that brief conversation at church showed me my fears. I was afraid of the opinions of others, and I was afraid of the trajectory of my daughter's life. I cared more about the opinions of others than I did about the opinion of God. I believed more in my fears than I trusted Him. My reactions weren't just a reflection of my tendency to worry. They were a reflection of my needing God.

Healing starts with acknowledging we're broken. Seeing God as Healer starts with seeing ourselves in need of healing.

And so God hides us. He takes us into a place where the opinions of others fail us. Where we can't see through our fears. That's where He speaks to us. And the longing that comes from being hidden makes us more aware of our brokenness, more receptive to His healing, than we'd ever be in the light of the world's applause.

The perfume was, indeed, a waste. As Mary's critics pointed out, she could have sold it and given the money to the poor. But Jesus defended Mary's sacrifice.

"She has done what she could," He said to the skeptics in the room. These are the words of a Savior in flesh who saw Mary's actions—and her woundedness—in a different light. He saw her not as one forever broken but as someone in need of healing who reached for that healing, beautifully. And He healed her as He spoke of her, transforming her sacrifice from waste to beauty.

Mary had an offering for Him who was healing her with Himself. We don't know the specifics about Mary's brokenness or the ways she needed this healing, this wholeness of Him. Perhaps in relationships, in destructive choices, in jealousy or fear. But Jesus had seen it all before that night. He sheltered her with how He spoke of her. He made her story part of the gospel story and gave her a leading role in His resurrection. And so it was Mary, with all of her history and all of her lack, who anointed Him for burial with her wasteful outpouring of fragrant oil. This once-broken woman now being healed prepared the Savior for His own healing—and for the healing of the world.

I was in my thirties before I ever acknowledged one of the most significant broken parts of my story: the loss of my dad.

My dad was my hero. He watched me run across a playground one day and told me over dinner that night, "Kid, you've got a stride. Let's teach you how to really run." A decade and a half later, I was still lacing my shoes for races. My dad drove ten hours to watch me finish my first marathon.

A vivid memory I have of my childhood living room is of my dad sitting with me and listening to my teenage angst. I didn't tire him. My dad loved processing life with me. As he drove me to drama class and voice lessons, he never once tried to talk me out of my dream of becoming an actress. My dad dreamed with me. He made life seem limitless.

But everything changed one hot August day when I was fourteen years old. I biked home from my best friend's house and found my dad slumped on the couch. A back injury had returned with a vengeance. Many surgeries later, my dad was no longer hitting the tennis ball with me or running laps with me around the block. He was wheelchair-bound and sleeping in a bed we'd lugged down to the first-floor family room.

I seemed to take it all in stride, as most of us do when our childhood tilts. "Children are resilient," they say. What they mean is, "Children learn to cope, until they can't anymore."

My dad and I stayed close. He could barely sleep the night before I got on a plane to backpack across Europe on a college summer break. He lived my adventures along with me, whether or not he was physically with me.

Dad died a young death from a quickly growing cancer a month after I turned thirty-two. But it wasn't until years later when I had five children and a full schedule and a mortgage that I realized what had happened when I was fourteen, how that time when my dad's body first broke had affected the way I saw my life from then on.

It was the hiddenness and loneliness of motherhood that slowed me down enough to notice. With five boisterous kids and no one else noticing my days, I saw it—that my search for approval from older leaders was a hunger for my dad's validation, something he wasn't able to give in the years I needed it most. I had spent much of my early-adult life running harder, working to achieve more, and pushing myself further—all in an effort to get the smile I wanted from my dad, who was gone. Even years after his death, as a new mom, I was still reaching out for approval and validation, but at two o'clock on a Tuesday afternoon, no affirming adults were around to give it. God hid me from the approving eyes I sought so that I could find His.

Over weeks and months of talking with God about the loss I'd learned to stuff deep, God spoke into my wounds. (It doesn't always happen in a single afternoon like it did that day with my daughter under the Ugandan sun.) He reminded me that He saw me during those years of my dad's broken body. He had words of validation for me in Scripture that made my heart come alive. They far surpassed words that even the most trusted leader might say or the approving nod of the one whose affirmation I most wanted.

God called me to healing even after I thought I was already healed. *Hadn't I grieved my dad when he died?* I wondered. I'd always said I'd grieved for my dad even before he died, as he endured a long and painful decline. What I couldn't see, and what was perhaps more accurate, is that I had never grieved for my dad's *life*.

The tears came. How was it possible that my dad had been out of my life for so many years and it wasn't until now that I desperately wanted to remember everything about him? The scents of sweat and fried eggs that filled our kitchen on childhood Saturday mornings after my dad returned from playing tennis with his buddies. The safety I felt as a young girl having him kneel beside my bed and fill my mind with stories that gave flight to my imagination. The thrill of sharing a raft with him in the ocean, riding waves twice my size but not feeling the least bit fearful because of who I was with.

Why did this happen to me, God? I choked out with guttural cries.

And God peeled away a layer from the part of my heart where I'd buried my dad without grieving him, where I'd never grieved the parts of my childhood and young adulthood that were lost to the injury that took him—as we knew him— from us.

God wasn't working to heal me so that I could "be healed"

and be more readily useful to Him. He was healing me so that I would know Him as Healer. He was moving in, to me, in the healing. I was raw in this place of experiencing old pain that had hung like low clouds over my life. But when I saw God as Healer, my broken pieces didn't feel so daunting or heavy. I wanted to bring them to Him because I saw Him respond out of who He is. I wanted more of the nearness I felt when I broke before Him.

When our wounds meet the Healer, we begin to live from new places of restoration instead of just working to avoid these old aches. Isaiah wrote this of the Healer:

> He has sent Me to heal the brokenhearted . . .
> To give them beauty for ashes,
> The oil of joy for mourning,
> The garment of praise for the spirit of heaviness;
> That they may be called trees of righteousness,
> The planting of the LORD, that He may be glorified.
>
> —ISAIAH 61:1, 3

We grow tall as we heal, as we recognize our need for healing, as we allow ourselves to be thirsty, digging our roots deep into unseen places.

I'm a frequent and vivid dreamer, but I hadn't had even one dream of substance of my dad since his burial until years later when I finally allowed myself to grieve him.

I dreamed I was meeting with an influential person about my first book, which had recently been published. I'd gone to this person's estate at his request and was nervously answering his questions. From across the room, I spotted a man in his thirties with a familiar head of red hair, young and handsome and confident. He looked at me and in an instant I knew it was my father—my dad, the tennis coach and teacher and vibrant grasper of life I remember most. He was the age that he had been when I was seven or eight, during my golden years of childhood when the carpet beside my bed was permanently indented by his knees from tucking me in at night.

When my eye caught his, he didn't say a word. He moved no closer to me. He just smiled the knowing yet proud smile that a father gives only to his daughter or son.

And he winked.

Then he was gone, along with the dream. I was fully awake at three in the morning. Undone. I'd seen my dad again, the dad I remember. He'd entered into the conversation in my life that was most vulnerable at that time—my creativity, my story, set out for others to see and criticize as they wished.

This is the dad who set up a folding chair at every one of my footraces, yet wasn't there when my book was published five years and one day after his death.

In my vulnerable expression of creativity, I needed a daddy's approval. I needed God's approval. But I didn't realize my need for God's affirmation right here, my desperation, until I received it through that dream. God responded to my grief, to my blubbering laments, in a way that brought healing to a whole stretch of life my dad hadn't seen on earth.

When we acknowledge the parts of us that are broken, we have significant growth spurts in God. As I grieved the loss of my dad, God was tender, personal, and patient. I grew as I gave myself permission to grieve—long past the time I'd allotted for grieving—and God healed with His presence over that moment and that slivered part of my heart. The long-broken parts of me don't disqualify me from His love. Instead, they catch His eye. He heals us—from the inside out.

——————— *For Your Continued Pursuit* ———————

Psalm 19:12 | Psalm 34:18 | Psalm 51:1–17 | Psalm 139:1–10 | Psalm 147:3 | Proverbs 23:10–11 | Song of Songs 2:3 | Isaiah 55:8–9 | Isaiah 61:1, 3 | Ezekiel 47:12 | Mark 14:3–9 | John 1:4–5 | Revelation 22:2

twelve

HOLY WHISPERS

Embracing the Mysteries of God

"She has kept this for the day of My burial."

—JOHN 12:7

It is 4:09 p.m. My children are quiet, tucked away in the back loft playing. The babe is sure to sleep another thirty minutes at least. I'd penciled in four o'clock as my time to step away and breathe, my "wonder hour." But now it's nine minutes past four and my tasks are haunting me. These are the two busiest weeks of my spring. I'd been watching them approach on the calendar for months. Easter is a tick away, and twenty people will be joining us for our annual Passover Seder dinner. There are two impending speaking engagements to prep for and a manuscript deadline just around the corner. Rest feels like an undeserved luxury.

But I close the laptop and close the office doors and step outside, away from all the reminders of what is left undone. I lace my running shoes and hit the trail for a walk through the nature preserve adjacent to our house.

It is 70 degrees in March, and I hear the noises of spring:

My feet crunching against wintered crabgrass speckled with new green. The woodpecker hammering somewhere above me. The rabbit moving through the brush.

I hear my heart too.

I feel God here. Rather, I feel *known* here, tromping through the woods without a soul in sight. I pass the stream near our property and I'm fairly certain that, other than a hunter or two, no one but us has looked at that stream in the past year. It's hidden, and so am I.

I notice the Bradford pear is in bloom on the other side of the loop I'm walking. The tree is striking against the brown of winter, holding thousands of white cotton balls from its limbs. I didn't notice it last year as it produced its fruit alongside the rest of the forest's compatriots. This year it is a loner. And brilliant.

We're all hidden, together, under His eye, these winter-ized trees and me. Masked, tucked away this afternoon, yet seen and thriving. He sees me and I know He sees me, and *this* reality, made clearer in the quiet of the afternoon, makes me want to talk to God. I want to participate in what was once discipline and is now the tender cord, drawn tighter and tighter, that connects me to the one who made me and knows me.

Waiting back at home is a hungry toddler, starting the roll call he does after every afternoon nap. "Mommy, Daddy, Caleb, Lily . . ."

Waiting back at home is an impossible list of tasks. I'd be superhuman to complete it, yet it's still written in Pilot ink on a notecard on my desk.

Waiting back at home are all the ingredients for dinner. The meat has been thawing for hours, dripping off the counter and onto the hardwood floor. I stepped over the pooling red to walk outside.

So many untended pieces of my life are waiting for me, just as they'll be waiting again tomorrow. I'll handle each one better because of what is happening on my insides out here in the wilderness of the walking trail.

These times of peace and conversation with God in the midst of a full-tilt life are not the waste I once thought they were. I started talking to God when I was hidden and hungry, and found the key that unlocks the deepest joy of any life: secret prayer. Whispers with God. My faith hinges upon this. His Word doesn't work its way inside of me unless it becomes my dialogue with Him. The gospel doesn't spread from my heart to my hands unless He's directly informing it. No relationship, covenanted or not, can grow without time, face to face.

I come alive in this conversation. I hear His heart here. And I change here. These moments have become the greatest thrill, the greatest adventure, of my life.

As I walk, I unload my heart to God. Phrases from His Word echo through my mind, intersecting with my sighs before God, reminding me that He knows what He made in me. I can't imagine that responding to one more email or getting a head start on dinner or finally scraping off of the pantry shelf the dried honey that's been driving me crazy could be as good or as needed as this. One more social media post can never settle me as much as exhaling my thoughts before God. I want—I need—to talk to God when no one is looking. I thrive on what happens there. *I do love this Jesus.*

Some things that I will ask of Him, no one will ever see or know or hear. "The secret of the LORD is with those who fear Him," we read in the Psalms (Ps. 25:14). Pouring out my thoughts to Him and carrying the thoughts of His heart toward me, and toward my family and the people in my world, is not merely a part of life in God. It is *all* of life in God.

Just before I make the last turn on the trail and head back to our yard, I pass the back side of the lonely Bradford pear. There, in the middle of what is still winter wilderness, is glorious spring. Hidden and beautiful.

I've come to believe that familiarity is the enemy of anyone who wants to fall in love with God.

The faith leaders in Jesus' day were so familiar with and attached to their version of religion and their expectations of the Messiah that they put nails through the hands of the best thing that ever happened to them. Even Jesus' closest companions were trapped in their ways of thinking and seeing things. He repeatedly gave them insights about the kingdom and what was to come, but they couldn't see beyond the temporal—the visible and the familiar. Only a few had a sense of what His words really meant and of the darkness, and the light, to come. Mary was one of the few.

We don't know whether Mary chose to pour out the oil at Jesus' feet because she knew His death was certain and imminent. We do know that Mary was immersed in the traditions of her culture, including the respectful anointing of honored guests and the anointing of the dead in preparation for burial. Feasting and grieving. Mary would know the rituals and cultural expectations for both.

"She has kept this for the day of My burial," Jesus said of Mary and her fragrant oil (John 12:7). His words suggest that Mary understood His heart and His future in a way that only those who are intimate with God can.

Mary's connectedness to Jesus was both private—love spilled—and public. Soon, the Son of God would shed His humanity, the humanity He took up for everyone around that table, for Mary, and for her family's forever-descendants. The oil Mary poured was His transitional robe.

Mary participated in God's biggest story by following a holy nudge inside her, one that grew from her time with Him. It was all she could do. It is all God calls us to do.

Much like the faith leaders and even those nearest disciples of Jesus' time, we too are at risk of missing Jesus, of failing to see who He really is, because of our attachments to the safe things we think we already understand about Him. Pastor Eugene Peterson describes it this way: "Left to ourselves, we will pray to some god who speaks what we like hearing, or to the part of God we manage to understand. But what is critical is that we speak to the God who speaks to us, and to everything that he speaks to us."[15] We allow ourselves to be lulled into a dull familiarity with the parts of Jesus we've experienced, the passages in His Word we've studied most, the truths about Him we can explain and understand. Then we string all of these familiar things together and call them God. And when we pray from this place of familiarity, instead of being alert for how the truth of how He really is will likely upend our human understanding, we end up watching for confirmation of what we already know.

It's here that prayer becomes stale and sends us searching elsewhere for adventure. But God brings us back to the simple accessibility of prayer—the hinge of our relationship with Him—and invites us to pray like wide-eyed children.

An airplane in the sky is a "jumping car" to my two-and-a-half-year-old, who is just beginning to make sense of the world. In God's invitation for us to come to Him as children, He understands that we likely will behave in similar ways by using what we know and recognize to make sense of what we don't yet know and can't yet see about Him.

This is how finite humanity approaches the infinite God.

Yet true growth in God requires that our perspective of Him grow with us. Progressively, prayer becomes less about relating to Him as we're certain He must be and more about seeing His bigness in light of how small and limited we are. We ask more questions, expect more mystery, leave more room for God to overturn our understanding. It's in this growth that we gladly exchange familiarity with God for the unknowns and His surprises.

The ones who lean into hiddenness begin to see that conversation with God has more to do with a growing connectedness to His heart and less to do with getting the answer we want. These prayers often begin with words like, "God, I barely know You and I want to know You more. My life is found in connecting to You, not in following what I think I already know about You."

That's when we know we've left milk behind and are dining on the meat of maturity in God.

"I just heard the baby's heartbeat," she whispered as she scooted from the church aisle into a seat just next to mine.

This mom-to-be had just graduated from her first trimester and was bubbling over with new data points on her unseen little one. But as her words and her enthusiasm moved past my mind into my heart, grief crowded in. At the time, we were still waiting for our older two daughters to come home.

With Eden and Caleb, I'd never before known parenthood. I hadn't thought I'd care about things like baby yawns and toddler babble, the silly observations children make and the wide-eyed way they navigate ordinary life. I lived in the present as I anticipated their arrival, wondering when the next piece of paperwork would clear so that we could travel to get them.

After these beloved two were home, a whole new sensory side of parenting opened up to me. I loved the smell of Eden's skin and the softness of her hair after a bath. I loved rubbing each of Caleb's unusually pliable ears between my fingers. These children were *mine*, and I was growing to love the parts of them I'd not considered when I held only a glossy photograph in my hand.

With Lily and Hope, it was harder to wait because now I knew what I was missing. Each day they lived across the ocean was another day I wasn't holding them. I wasn't tending to their little-girl skin. I couldn't picture how tall Lily would stand against my shoulders or how much of Hope's body I could enfold within my arms.

So I made a new kind of baby book for these two who had already left babyhood behind. I started talking to God about what I didn't know. I made what was unfamiliar to me the starting point for our dialogue. I asked for His heart for these girls.

What would You have me pray?

This God had made our girls in secret, when no one was watching or recording or perhaps even celebrating. He knew every single moment of my children's undocumented lives. So I asked Him for insights about their personalities. This dialogue with God wasn't one of many parts of my relationship with my children—it was the only bloodline I had. I learned motherhood of them by talking to God first. Through words of Scripture, He showed me their heartbeat. I prayed into what I couldn't see, and because of what I couldn't see, I prayed with His eyes.

Lily and Hope were spending their nights in cramped rooms lined with beds without anyone to kiss them goodnight. I was on another continent asking God for prayers about them to pray back to Him. I prayed His Word, His promises, His ideas for my girls. As I prayed for children I'd never met,

I developed a new depth in my relationship with God. Instead of a growing girth, I had a growing connectedness to God.

God was teaching me about the weight that prayer holds in His unseen world. No one saw those prayers. I couldn't take snapshots of my inner life in God to post in social media feeds. Even on these pages, I can only reference them. I can't truly share them.

What was masked, what was unfamiliar, was unveiled in my private conversations with God. My prayers directed toward the unseen, my prayers in hiddenness, were as real to me as a heartbeat on a sonogram screen.

We'll mature without effort into wrinkles and gray hair, but our hearts won't mature deep into God by default. We have to desire more and more of God. Paul prayed for such greater fullness in our experience of God: "[I pray] that you, being rooted and grounded in love, may be able to comprehend with all the saints what is the width and length and depth and height—to know the love of Christ which passes knowledge; that you may be filled with all the fullness of God" (Eph. 3:17–19).

There is a *further* filling to those who already have committed their lives to following Jesus, a filling that comes as a result of sinking our roots ever deeper into Him—His is a love our minds can't fully understand.

Prayer—conversation with God—is how we sink our roots into what is real and will last forever. Prayer fights against the vaporlike existence of a life rooted only in what others see, which is gone just after we show and tell. Prayer laces our hearts to the unseen mysterious God, to whom we say, *Who You are, God, is more important than what I see in front of me and what others see of me.*

No one but God sees in full this glorious exchange that produces deep and lasting growth. Prayer tethers us to the truest reality, one that will never change. His.

I published my story on paper a few years back and entered into a whole new world of metrics. I bled on the page, and now I saw there were ways to measure its impact or lack thereof.

Had I wanted to, I could have compared the sales rank of my book with that of every other published author at any given time of the day. A few more clicks and I could count all the reviews as they came in. I could read the words of those who loved the book and those who felt otherwise. I could click through social media tags and images and comments to analyze from every angle what people were saying about the outpouring of my heart. And by any of these metrics, my book would have been merely that: what I could see and measure with my eyes.

But I wanted another measure. I wanted to birth this book with my nervous hand in His, leaning more into what I couldn't see than what I could. So I prayed prayers that only God and I (and sometimes Nate) knew about. I prayed wild prayers for this baby book, much like the ones I prayed for my girls when they were still in Uganda (which is when I learned that prayers make the best kind of baby books).

This exchange with God became more important to me than His answers. I knew He *could* answer—He was able—and I was also beginning to trust His leadership enough to know that when He didn't answer, it was all right.

Most of all, I wanted to dream *with* Him. *His* dreams, His way. Bigger dreams than I could conceive from looking around me.

I wanted to just talk to Him about the *whole* thing. I wanted to talk to Him about the eyes that might read the pages and the people who would pass dogeared copies on to friends. I wanted to pour out my fears to Him and hear His tender response, to find the gentle side of Him in His Word and carefully affix it to each one of my crazy nerves. I wanted to ask big things of Him, and I wanted to pray for the tiny details—the cover, the design, the font. And I wanted to align with Him: I wanted to know His heart, His thoughts, His dreams for this book.

It's what you do with a best friend and a father and an invested coach. God was all of these to me and more. I wanted to pray my way through God's nature and not just read about it in the pages of His book. I wanted to see it cropping up all over my own story.

I did. And He did. I cry-prayed and talked and gushed and fretted, out loud and right to Him. And He winked. Just like my dad in my dream, God winked. He responded in ways I wouldn't have had an eye for had I not prayed them first. Prayer positioned me to notice. *Him.*

Some of these conversations with God on the inside happened as I faced the critical eyes of others on the outside, eyes that made me want to quit and never write another word because it hurt too much to take creative risks like this.

But what kept me moving forward was that there was this second storyline, the most important storyline. The first might have been "Sara published a book," peppered with pretty images of the teal cover and people's stories of how they'd been touched by it. But the second storyline has a title that I can't share even here or it might lose its weight and beauty. And all the images that stretch across my mind as I write about it are mostly to be shared between God and me.

I needed the second storyline in order to walk out the first.

The wink of God: It comes when we believe He is capable of reaching tenderly and knowingly into our story. It comes when we believe He wants to intertwine His story with ours and tell our story back to us, His way.

This is prayer. It is coming to God, opening His Word, expecting His whisper and dialoguing with Him, knowing that there are myriad sides of Him yet to be explored.

Prayer is sinking deeply into the soil of God and expecting to be nourished in ways that are mostly undetectable to the human eye.

God made us in secret. We grow in secret. But that secret space is not a void. He stays in the secret, right there with us. That's where we grow, deep.

∞

When I was newly on full-time staff with the high school ministry and just out of college, I gave my first gospel presentation in a new city to a roomful of sweaty teenagers from all over the city. While I was speaking, most of the two hundred kids stared at me blankly or cast zoned-out looks elsewhere or flirted with their neighbors. Only a few of the leader-types in the room looked like they were actually listening. I was upfront, passionate, and felt virtually unnoticed.

I can still feel the heavy weight that lodged in my stomach as I lugged the overhead projector back to our ministry office after the night was over. I spent the drive back to the office analyzing my twelve-minute talk from twelve different angles. I knew I had bombed.

For weeks afterward, my face flushed when I thought about it. *Never again*, I vowed. I'd work ten times harder for the next one, ten times harder to ensure I wouldn't say something stupid or repeat words that weren't received.

This talk was about them and me. I hadn't considered, at twenty-two, that it was the power of God, not my words, that could change a human heart, or that fruit came from my abiding in Him, not from my perfect delivery.

So I worked hard on my delivery, mostly so that I wouldn't ever again feel the shame of vulnerability. I didn't consider then that God uses foolish things to make His name known. I just wanted never to be foolish again.

Fifteen years later, I was speaking to another crowd. I was talking about a passion for pursuing God in the midst of family life. I'd spoken publicly many times before, but I'd not yet fully shed the fear that I might walk out of a room having bombed.

I'd spent weeks in advance praying about this particular conference, asking God to relieve the fear of failure, the fear of saying it wrong or missing His leadership or finding myself shamed. It'd been a long time since I was twenty-two, but there was still this thread of fear entwined in my preparation to speak.

After my talk, I stepped off the stage, spoke with a few people, and then walked to the car with Nate. I was feeling increasingly drawn to hiddenness since I'd felt more and more exposed after writing my book. I wanted to get back to those secret conversations with God. I wanted to live hidden, no matter how my talks and interviews and the book might expose me.

As Nate and I climbed into the car on that overcast afternoon, my first thoughts were leading me into shame. But instead of allowing them free rein, I asked God, *What did You think?*

This was about us was the phrase I felt rise up within my spirit.

God told me what I already knew, but what I needed to hear again: the story of God and me is my most significant story. His eyes on me and into my life are the source from which I draw everything else. Whether I am folding laundry or speaking from a platform, my exchanges with God are always about His reach for me and my reach for Him in return, again and again. The rest of life is the overflow.

Prayer, this internal exchange with God, is where it all happens.

Underground.

Rooting down deeper still in Him.

And eventually growing up.

——————— *For Your Continued Pursuit* ———————

Psalm 25:14 | Psalm 81:7 | Psalm 139 | Ezekiel 36:26–27 | Matthew 6:4–6 | Matthew 18:3 | John 15:1–7 | 1 Corinthians 1:27–29 | 1 Corinthians 2:9 | Ephesians 3:16–21 | Hebrews 5:12–14 | Hebrews 6:19–20

thirteen

THE HIDDEN WAY

Becoming a Friend of God

"Wherever this gospel is preached
throughout the world, what she has done
will also be told, in memory of her."

—MATTHEW 26:13 NIV

The darkness of the Christmas Eve sky contrasted with the streets below, all of them aflame. Strings of multicolored lights and inflatable snowmen and light-skinned Marys and Josephs lit the night.

This was Lily and Hope's first American Christmas, and part of me wanted to keep them inside, to keep their eyes innocently fixed on a miraculous birth and the unsuspecting shepherds and the world's greatest gift of God come as a human. We drove to the Christmas Eve service, and their mouths formed steam on the windows as they ogled plastic Santas and luminaries and LED icicles.

This was the first Christmas Eve service I could remember in which the children were invited to come forward, mid-service. I hadn't prepared mine. Things that most children handle easily can dislodge children like mine, whose lives have already had a deeper dislodging.

All but one of my children went up front, joining one hundred of their peers, many of whom looked a bit nervous as they faced an audience of onlookers and parents snapping photos and mouthing "smile" to the little people they had made.

There was a boisterous dad up front, leading the children, coaching them with questions through a retelling of the nativity story. Arms shot up and out even before the next question was asked. Kids were loaded, ready. Each child wanted his or her voice heard.

The designated dad closed with one last question: "Now, what did the angels say?" And my child, who had raised her hand to answer every single question just like every other eager-to-participate little one, finally had her number called.

The dad in charge pointed to her, my little girl who'd been in America for only a few months and who pantomimed more than she spoke. I still wasn't sure if she understood that the plastic snowmen weren't a part of what happened that first Christmas.

She responded confidently by reciting verses we happened to have spent the last few months memorizing—the only complete sentences in her memory bank, and full of words whose meaning she didn't know: "Then the angel said to them, 'Do not be afraid, for behold, I bring you good tidings of great joy which will be to all people. For there is born to you this day in the city of David a Savior, who is Christ the Lord'" (Luke 2:10–11).

The room full of parents and grandparents and friends

erupted with cheers. My little girl about burst out of her dress. She did it! Whatever *it* was.

She ran back into my arms and I cried.

I wasn't crying because I was the proud mama whose child had given the winning answer. This wasn't a moment to display the stellar memorization skills we'd imparted or even the fact that we were memorizing Scripture in our home.

The others in that room didn't know where my little girl had been eating her meals a year before or that she'd missed more than a few. They weren't close enough to see that I still had African dirt underneath my fingernails from a summer of clawing through paperwork walls to get her home. They didn't see what I saw. They couldn't have. They weren't meant to, at least not in that moment.

But the thirty seconds between when the crowd erupted around her and she bolted back into my arms were holy moments. Through my daughter's words that evening, God reached into the deepest part of me and said, *I see you.*

No one in that room, apart from Nate, knew the inner dialogue I'd been having recently. Overnight, we had gone from two children to four, and sometimes it felt like we were carrying the burdens of twelve with all the years of loss they bore. Most days, I felt like I was drowning in their brokenness. Hearts take time to heal, certainly more time than I had allotted or expected.

As I reeled from the body blows of all the ways their losses impacted everything from our dinner times to afternoon play dates—and what it would mean for them in the years ahead—I wanted other people to feel the pain too. I wanted friends to know how hard it was to show up to church on time or to convince this young one to step away from the wall during ballet class or to teach another one to look adults in the eye (after she'd spent an orphanage lifetime learning to look away). I wanted family to see that typical gatherings sometimes couldn't run as planned, that I couldn't prepare for what might trigger an angry reaction or when grief might suddenly overtake a child.

Someone, anyone, please notice. Or rather, *Someone, anyone— know.*

I wanted to shout it everywhere we went: "Behind this child is a story!" And maybe the truer statement I wanted to shout was, "Behind this woman is a story!"

But that Christmas Eve night, the ancient announcement rolling off my daughter's lips was a better gift than a whole throng of onlookers who *noticed* and *knew.* "And your Father who sees in secret will reward you openly" (Matt. 6:18) speaks both of the one who sees in secret and the parts of us that were made for rewarding.

He *does* reward.

It would be disingenuous for me to say that I didn't want any reward for the outpouring I'd given to these children who, in their aches and losses, sometimes boiled over with anger and other times stewed in sullen unresponsiveness. I'd be dishonest if I said I didn't need anyone to notice that I'd been cleaning up emotional wreckage I didn't cause, only to do it again the next day. I'd be superhuman to say I could thrive for days, much less hours, mending heart-ouchies without an acknowledging nod in my direction.

At the very least, I wanted someone to thank me for making dinner.

I'm adult enough to know that the proverbial nod from even the most respected person is a vapor that soon vanishes, but I'm child enough to feel the need for an eye, an intimate whisper of acknowledgment, a "Way to go!" note from a friend. So I can get stuck between these two: serving without a desire for recognition, all the while clamoring internally for my outpouring to be known.

My daughter's words that night were God's way of saying to me, *I saw the hundreds of minutes before this one when she bristled against your loving leadership, and I'm at work in her.*

This is God, my friend. The one who *knows* me. The one who *gets* me.

"How precious also are Your thoughts to me, O God! How great is the sum of them!" (Ps. 139:17). When I don't realize what I'm truly craving, God's thoughts toward me will get lost while I seek affirmation from a sea of other eyes. But when I listen in hiddenness, God's thoughts reveal themselves and become precious. My hearing, trained in that hiddenness, becomes attuned to the best kind of sound: the voice of my friend.

Throughout history, God related to many of His people as friends. He sought friends too. God searched the earth for those who *got* Him.

"And he was called the friend of God," James says of

Abraham, after stating, "Abraham believed God, and it was accounted to him for righteousness" (James 2:23).

Abraham's descendants were identified as those who came from the forever friend of God: "descendants of Abraham Your friend forever" (2 Chron. 20:7).

John the Baptist referred to himself as the "friend of the bridegroom" (John 3:29).

And lest we think this friend status is reserved for the superheroes of the faith, we can turn to Jesus' words to all His followers: "No longer do I call you servants, for a servant does not know what his master is doing; but I have called you friends, for all things that I heard from My Father I have made known to you" (John 15:15). A friendship that started between Father and Son expanded to include you and me.

Yes, we want to be known. But how often do we consider that God wants to be known too? The unsearchable God does invite our searching; friendship is formed in this seeking. God wants to be our friend in the way that friends share more than high-fives and occasional help. He wants to share hearts and stories and inner lives.

This friendship with God isn't just about the winks He gives to us when no one is looking. He's also searching the earth for ones who will look back, who will *know* Him, who will carry His heart.

I first discovered that I wanted to be one of those friends when He met me in my hidden years of barrenness. Over time, the women around me who had experienced barrenness for as many years as I had grew fewer and fewer. Yet as human friends who understood this pain diminished, I found an understanding friend in God, the kind of friend who made me want even deeper friendship. More reaching.

I wanted to be a friend *to* God.

They clamored for Jesus, perhaps more desperate for healing than for a Healer.

The curious and accusatory and hungry, they thronged Him.

Those nearest to Him, the ones He invited close, fought for a seat at His right hand. Even the ones who knew Him best glommed on to His fame.

To some, He was a miracle, and to others a fraud. But wherever Jesus went, opinions and needs followed Him. He came to save the world, and the world let out its cry when it saw Him.

But Mary was different.

Wasteful with her love.

The others around the table likely counted their money and ministry impact, but she had thought that she might carry His burden with Him. She reached toward Him in friendship. And He spoke on her behalf. He chose her, the woman from the back row, to memorialize.

This is the memorial, told throughout all of time: Mary befriended God.

And the gospel would no longer be told without sharing the story of the woman so enraptured by God that she wasted all she had on Him. That she became His friend.

A few years ago, I was invited to speak to a house full of women for an overnight retreat. I'd held a microphone a few times in the year or two before then, but I still had nerves when I stood up in front of people. It had been a long time since the ministry days of my twenties, when I was frequently speaking or leading a Bible study in front of a crowd.

Now I was about to spend a weekend speaking to twenty or so women I didn't know, young adults in trendy jeans and fortysomething moms who could still hang with those half their age, all congregated in one lakehouse over food and stories and a shared hunger for God.

I arrived that first night with a nursing babe and my eldest daughter as a helper. I was tired from traveling and uncertain how I'd do the next twenty-four hours with two children in tow. I tucked in Bo and meandered with the women down to the lake for the first session. We'd meet waterside as the sun set.

With the chairs circled up, I began to speak. As I moved through my notes, the sun dropped behind the treeline at my back on the other side of the lake. The day went from dusk to dark in what felt like minutes. This transition left me feeling suddenly alone.

I could see nothing but the dim lights from the kitchen of the lakehouse up on the hill. I couldn't even make out the silhouettes of the women around me. My notes, too, were lost in the darkness.

I had no idea whether my audience was moved by this

message or if they were quietly nodding off. I had no eye contact cues to guide my words. And I had no idea how much was left in what I'd planned to say. I was winging it from memory and by the whispers of God inside of me. The only lines in my Bible I could use were the ones I'd memorized.

So I delivered a talk to the crickets and the bullfrogs and the owls, the most responsive of the crew around me.

Afterward, as I walked up the hill and back to my room, my mind launched into critique mode, combing through my talk for any mishap or hiccup. Just a few more moments of this and I would go under. I knew this shame spiral routine by heart. I'd been here before.

So I stopped. I asked the Lord to breathe His love into this perplexing night. And then it hit me. In an instant I knew this night would be the image I'd carry with me into every public speaking engagement for years to come.

The pitch-black night had given me a new light.

God let the night drop over my vision so that I would search His heart alone, so I would seek His thoughts for these women. Their nodding expressions, warmly encouraging me as I spoke, were not as significant as His heartbeat for them, a heartbeat He might share with me if I turned my eyes toward Him instead.

This is friendship with God.

He sees me when no one is looking, and I search Him in response.

Perhaps God initiates friendship with a desire that we might befriend Him, eagerly, in return.

John the Baptist, in calling himself the "friend of the

bridegroom," qualifies this friendship as one who "stands and hears him." Who "rejoices greatly because of the bridegroom's voice" (John 3:29–30). Friendship with God means hearing. We become God's friend when we listen for His heart and His soft whisper in His Word.

Like Mary, we can tend to God—listening, tuning our ears to the cadence of His heartbeat, and spilling out our lives in response to what we hear. This is communion. Surrender of our lives, unto Him. He made us for this.

Author Jon Bloom writes that Mary's pouring out her perfume wasn't a waste but a windfall: "A poured-out life of love for Jesus that counts worldly gain as loss displays how precious he really is. It preaches to a bewildered, disdainful world that Christ is gain and the real waste is gaining the world's perfume while losing one's soul."[16]

I want to be another Mary.

I want to know God as a precious friend.

My sweet daughter was recently praying for my book. *This* book. Though she didn't know what it was about, she knew I sometimes took time away to write. She asked God for His eyes for me as she prayed. Then she looked up from underneath those dainty eyelids and said, "Mommy, you're like a morning glory, except you open in the night when no one sees you but God. And you're hidden and closed during the day."

The morning glory in our yard has always enamored my kids as they've tried to catch it when it is closed and figure out exactly when it opens. Now this mysterious flower was a picture for me. Of me.

I want God to get the best of me. Unfurled and reaching. Exposed but tender. Whether in the dark or light. Open to Him.

I sat in another circle of women in a different state and a different setting and heard one woman say about prayer, "I know I *should* pray more, but it's so hard to live that out in the middle of the day." She is right, both about the call to prayer and about how most Christians see that call.

We're not merely invited to pray, but we are called to pray unceasingly. Always. In every circumstance and in every setting. On our back patio pruning geraniums and in the laundry room loading the washer with whites and taking a shower and stretching at the gym and during that quick afternoon grocery stop and in the drive-through at Starbucks and sitting on the metal chairs at the DMV.

That's praying without ceasing. That's the kind of conversation with God that Paul says is possible: "Rejoice always, pray without ceasing, in everything give thanks; for this is the will of God in Christ Jesus for you" (1 Thess. 5:16–18).

As you read, do you feel your pulse rising? Just like the woman in the circle, are you pleading in defense of yourself in the way we often do when we see a gap, *This is really hard! I should have prayed more today, but how am I supposed to remember and find the time?*

But there is no need to plead or to defend. The gaps in our prayer lives are simply reasons to pause. To examine.

Though discipline is not a bad word, and certainly there are many times when discipline carries us when our fickle hearts won't, our prayerlessness reveals much more than a lack of stick-to-itiveness.

Paul, who wrote these words about unceasing prayer, was a friend of God. He wasn't a stalwart follower, more disciplined than the rest of us. God had been *near* to him. Near enough to share His secrets with Paul. God had to be such a close friend to Paul, perhaps at least in part because this man was out of other options: "From the Jews five times I received forty stripes minus one. Three times I was beaten with rods; once I was stoned; three times I was shipwrecked; a night and a day I have been in the deep; in journeys often, in perils of waters, in perils of robbers, in perils of my own countrymen, in perils of the Gentiles, in perils in the city, in perils in the wilderness, in perils in the sea, in perils among false brethren; in weariness and toil, in sleeplessness often, in hunger and thirst, in fastings often, in cold and nakedness" (2 Cor. 11:24–27).

Comrades turned traitors, accusing words, hurled stones, hunger, sleeplessness, brutal treatment by his countrymen, and untold perils. When he had no one and nothing else, Paul found a friend in God. God, in return, shared His secrets with His friend. Paul speaks of himself here: "And I know such a man—whether in the body or out of the body I do not know, God knows—how he was caught up into Paradise and heard inexpressible words, which it is not lawful for a man to utter" (2 Cor. 12:3–4).

Paul carved a friendship out of those mysterious whispers. This is holy and other, and yet Paul's true friendship with God was forged in circumstances that hid him and made him (in the world's eyes) not only an absolute fool but also a target for abuse—and worse. Paul didn't pray because he *should*. Paul prayed because he'd grown—*grown*—to want nothing more.

Maturing in our friendship with God, the place where somewhere down deep we all want to be headed, means wanting nothing more than to talk to Him because of who He is to us in our weakest, most confounded moments. This is what fueled Paul's passion for God: "That I may know Him and the power of His resurrection, and the fellowship of His sufferings" (Phil. 3:10).

Unceasing prayer can grow to be something we do not because of discipline but because of friendship. Desire. It's where we're headed, if we'll let Him take us there.

This God bent low to gift a son into thirty years of obscurity. It isn't beyond Him to stretch His hand of friendship into the middle minutes of our day, the "Hey, can I open myself to you for this moment?" kind of friendship, so that we might see engaging with Him as the preeminent prize of our lives.

One day you just may *want* to pray without ceasing.

Who knows what you might hear.

It was a normal Tuesday morning, and I was relieved. The day before, I had just finished what I thought would be the last chapter of this book. I slid out the door into a chorus of birds. My shoelaces were double-knotted for one of my first spring runs—off the treadmill belt and onto the road.

The dark was still hovering. I wore my reflector vest as I crossed the street and turned right out of my driveway. I would run one mile and stop to stretch and then another mile before turning back. Habit.

On my way back, I hit a patch of water and mud and fell hard and awkward, my limbs flying in opposite directions. I lay crumpled on the sidewalk, unable to walk, surprised and embarrassed. Nate had to come drive me home.

Days and doctor appointments later, I got my diagnosis: broken ankle. I was charged not to drive or walk for two months. One little run, one little fall, and all my plans for spring were suddenly muddled.

I tried to keep things in perspective. I hadn't gotten a midnight phone call that someone I treasured was gone. The storm didn't lift my house off its foundation. The time expected for my ankle to heal was only eight weeks, after all. These are all things I told myself to quell the internal fit I was throwing about not being able to go on long Saturday morning runs or take meandering walks with my children or scoot away to a coffee shop for a couple of hours to write and sip chai. I was trying to coach myself to see things another way.

Except it wasn't working. Self-coaching never makes a lasting shift.

But something else did.

I remembered *her*. This woman who still intrigues me. This woman who didn't grudgingly spill her livelihood onto Jesus' feet while biting the inside of her cheek in resentment but quite literally poured out all that she had for Him.

She *wanted* to give it all.

Of course, everyone else in the room called it waste. Human nature can't comprehend this kind of surrender—a relinquishing of the things that matter most to us—to a mysterious God. We can't coach ourselves up to a better perspective, just a little bit higher until we reach something holy. (Though we try.)

We need a new way.

We need a new way to endure pain, both acute and mundane, to face the daily deaths we're offered in broken ankles and broken dishwashers and broken relationships when we wish we could just walk away. We need to journey through the hidden spaces of our lives with an expectation of victory, as if we really believe that these unnoticed moments matter.

We need a hidden way.

This way God has given us looks like waste from our earthbound perspective. It always will. The outpouring at His feet will never make sense to human eyes. No, not ever.

But what strikes me most about Mary is that she had practice. It appears from earlier biblical accounts that she had created what might be called a lifestyle of waste: "There is only one thing worth being concerned about. Mary has discovered it, and it will not be taken away from her" (Luke 10:42 NLT).

Mary found it: the *only* thing worth being concerned about in this life.

She found Him.

Mary didn't have one wild brush with God and run to tell this world about it. She got near to Him and she stayed. We might say it this way: Mary practiced being wasted. She made a lifestyle of it. Something kept her there.

In the days after breaking my ankle, I managed my home and was a mom to my children and maintained relationships, all from my couch and crutches. I also mentally catalogued all the things I was missing. First, I thought about how I was losing about a dozen Saturday morning runs. But then I realized that even bedtimes were on the list. I wouldn't be able to walk up the stairs to my children's bedrooms or lift my toddler into his crib. Nor would I be planting the garden we'd been planning for weeks.

I'd half wished I could say something like, "But I realize these losses were so small compared with what my children faced in their early years and what my girlfriend in another state is facing with her cancer and what my dear friend lost when her dad died." But those words were empty self-coaching for me.

The only thing that effectively lifts me out of the rut of complaint is knowing that Jesus isn't calling these unproductive two months in a cast a waste. He is calling them an invitation.

With a broken ankle and a house to run, there is still only one thing worth my greatest concern, according to Jesus. Insert your own story here: with a child who is behind in school, with a best friend who has betrayed you, with a promotion you didn't get, with a promotion you won only to find yourself in over your head, there is only one thing truly worthy of your concern, only one thing that will deeply satisfy you and thrill you, at times, beyond measure.

Jesus didn't refer to this one thing so that we would shove

our emotions and lift our chins and stiffen our lips. He said it of a woman who looked up at Him, weak and vulnerable and thirsty, and likely uncertain and nervous in her thirst. He said it of a woman who was simply trying to get close to Him, to the one thing she thought might meet the deepest craving of her heart.

He said it of me, in His invitation, an almost-forty-year-old finally quieting down after the newest internal tantrum: *Sara, remember Me, the one thing always available to fill you. Even this change won't take it from you.*

You could pattern a lifetime around this one. Because as we look deep into His eyes, nothing is wasted.

Like so many in middle America, I grew up under the Friday night lights.

First, I was the wide-eyed little sister, tagging along behind my big sister to the games and congregating with friends under the bleachers, taking mental notes on how older girls acted. Then I was the ardent fan, barely watching the score but making youthful celebrities out of the best players, shouting their names and their numbers. Then (finally) I was the uniformed participant, cheering the team all the way home to Cougar Lane on musky fall nights while the parking lot lights served as smoke machines against the fall frost, welcoming back our small-town heroes.

When I outgrew the stands as a student, I returned in the

name of ministry. On these nights, I was just another member of the community rallying in the city's centrifuge, loving my bundled-up neighbors in between shouting the names of seventeen-year-old athletes.

As a young married woman without kids, I had a different sort of Friday night lights. I spent Friday nights with friends, all of us circled around the table of our favorite restaurant under low lights, sharing lives between bites.

For all those years, Fridays were the social metronome of my life.

But then, several years into marriage, came one Friday that was different.

I was alone, but now by choice. My husband was out of town, and I wasn't afraid of the night or myself or who I might find when the house was empty.

I brewed a cup of tea and I opened the back door. Only the screen separated me from the intermittent sounds of the night.

I cracked open my Bible, except this time it wasn't out of duty. I wanted to be here. I was drawn to Him, this God-man who had seen me in my weakness and heard my whimpering and saw my reach for Him, amid all my flaws. I wanted to talk to God. Not because of a looming decision or a penance I felt was overdue. I was hungry, craving more than what even the best of hot appetizers or the town's fanfare or a night with my best friend could give me. God was new to me, ever unfolding. With every new glimpse of Him, I wanted more.

And something in me knew that this raw and desiring side

of me is what God wanted too. Desire drew me—and who I was when I desired Him. I was beginning to like who I was under His eye. The raw me. The real me.

I liked Him, and He liked what He'd made in me.

Perhaps it was similar to the desire that drew me to spend years of Friday nights with best friends. We're drawn to where we come alive, to where our passion takes flight. To where we are known. We want to be with those who know us and remind us of what we like about ourselves. Those who invite us to consider our lives as much bigger than what our eyes can see.

I knew that I once would have called this time—God, me, my Bible—a terrible waste. I wasn't making plans to change the world or contemplating a major decision or even asking for a personal breakthrough. I was sitting with God just to enjoy Him. And I wanted to stay just a little bit longer.

It was a night of mutual affection, and yet it still felt a little awkward, just like the beginning stages of any true friendship. Of course He knew all of me, but I was just beginning to learn that I was comfortable being known.

And I wanted more. More of Him. More of that version of me.

This night was both emptier and fuller than anything I'd experienced on a Friday night. No lights, no fanfare, no victory celebration. Just me, squandering time with God, picking up a conversation we'd build upon over a lifetime.

Wasting time.

I'm not sure I had ever felt His pleasure more.

--------- *For Your Continued Pursuit* ---------

1 Samuel 13:14 | 1 Chronicles 16:11 | 2 Chronicles 16:9 |
2 Chronicles 20:7 | Psalm 14:2 | Psalm 19:12 | Psalm 26:8 | Psalm 80
| Psalm 139:17 | Proverbs 25:2 | Ezekiel 36:26 | Matthew 6:16–18 |
Matthew 20:20–28 | Matthew 26:1–13 | Luke 10:38–42 | John 1:5
| John 3:22–36 | John 14:26 | John 15:15 | Acts 6:4 | Acts 13:22 |
1 Corinthians 1:20–31 | 1 Corinthians 15:58 | 2 Corinthians 5:17 |
2 Corinthians 11:24–27 | 2 Corinthians 12:3–4, 7–11 | Philippians
3:10, 12–14 | 1 Thessalonians 5:16–18 | James 2:23 | Revelation 21:5

ACKNOWLEDGMENTS

Isaac Newton wrote, "If I have accomplished anything of value it is because I have stood upon the shoulders of giants." My thinking on the notion of hiddenness has inadvertently been influenced by so many, even from centuries past, whose stories populate our bookshelves—writers, giants of the faith in shepherd's clothes, missionaries, common people who bled for Jesus with their lives and did it in hiding, all because they loved Him.

I owe much to these, and to the parking lot attendants, the grocery store baggers, and the sage mothers of many children (like my late friend, Claire DeLaura), and to Sue, Pat, Dara, Cindy, Val, Anne, Betty, Tonya, Jina, JoAnna, Katie, Joan, Cathy, Susan, Amy, Betsy, Julie, Beth, Andee, and many others who loved Him profoundly when no one was looking and of whom God gave me a glimpse.

In addition, not so ironically, my name is on the cover of this book because of so many others who served and loved fiercely, with only a few (if any) noticing.

To everyone at Yates and Yates, especially Mike Salisbury and Curtis and Karen Yates: I had no idea what an ever-unfolding gift you would be. You pastored us while advocating for this book and its message.

And the team at Zondervan, to name just a few: Alicia Kasen, Brian Phipps, Jennifer VerHage, Sandy Vander Zicht. You all have taken a process that could have been merely transactional and laced it with thoughtful ingenuity and heart. I'm honored to have had such a dream team not once but twice.

To Jana Muntsinger and Pamela McClure: Thank you for making this fun, while not at the expense of being professional and determined.

Elisa Stanford: I'm not sure I could write another book without you. I've learned more from you about writing than any degree could have afforded me, and have formed a treasured friendship in the meantime.

To Jefferson and Alyssa Bethke: Having your voice accompany this message is an honor. Your thoughtfulness with your lives demonstrates a layer of beautiful hiddenness that some might dismiss. But not me.

To Dave and Tracey Sliker: I know I'm not the only one who has benefited from your cheerleading, but I sure feel like I am. You have infused more courage into me than I could sufficiently give credit for. Thank you, Dave, for reading the manuscript with your gifted critical eye.

To Kristy Reid, Kelly Raudenbush, and Rachel Medefind: for offering gentle input early and helping to sharpen this message.

Lisa Jacobson: I prayed for years for a sage in my life who understood both of my passions—for writing for His glory, and for keeping precious the value of motherhood and home. What a gift to have had you mentoring me from a distance.

MT girls: Hannah Robinson, Cherish Smith, Annie Kawase, Mary Arntsen, Rachael Steel, Erica Nork, Telma Weisman. It's early as I write this. You've only gathered in my family room a few times, and I'm already feeling the fruit of your partnership. Your hearts and your hunger for Him make this team significantly more than I could have envisioned.

And of course, Mandie Joy Turner: Your eye and your skill are only part of what I love about working with you. Thank you for bringing humor, gravity, and friendship to this work.

Tim and Chris Willard: You live this message, and our dialogue has given fuel to my writing it. Here's to many more fireside chats—you by yours, and we by ours, across the telephone line—about Him and beauty and hiddenness.

Jen Stutzman, Elizabeth Wilkerson, Abby Anderson, Nicole Rice, Molly Harrington, Trina Rogers: Each one of you has graced my life with pieces of Him that I wouldn't know or hadn't seen without you. You make me belly laugh, and you give flight to these crazy writing dreams of mine (even—especially—as I face my fear of it all) at the most needed times. This book has your fingerprints all over it.

Sarah Markman, Eliza Joy Capps, Kinsey Thurlow, Amy Wicks, Heidi Meythaler: Girls, you've demonstrated with your lives what happens when friendship and prayer intersect. You truly have fought for my heart in my writing, my marriage, and my motherhood.

To Kelly Tarr: I can think of no one else who lives the

message of hiddenness in Him more earnestly and fervently than you. You are one of God's greatest gifts to me.

Mom: Your friendship is one of the very best parts of my life. I want to be like you when I grow up.

To the ones under my roof who see it all—my sin, my languishing over my writing and speaking, my long, scruffy days in pajamas and a topknot, my kitchen dance routines—and still cuddle with me: Lily, Hope, Eden, Caleb, Bo, and Virginia. You are my absolute joy, my favorite part of life. My world would be dull without each of you.

And Nate: Sixteen years in and it just keeps getting better. You give me courage to write, over and over again. This book is ours, and this message is one that you live more wildly than I could ever hope to myself.

Last and greatest in my heart: Jesus. You've bored through my soul with the safest eyes I've ever known, and I keep wanting more. Your undoing is healing me.

NOTES

1. Dallas Willard, *The Divine Conspiracy: Rediscovering Our Hidden Life in God* (San Francisco: HarperSanFrancisco, 1998), 15.

2. Charles H. Spurgeon, *The Treasury of David*, vol. 3 (Massachusetts: Hendrickson, 1869), 263.

3. A. W. Tozer, *The Root of the Righteous* (Harrisburg, PA: Christian Publications, 1955), 50.

4. Dr. Dan Allender and Dr. Tremper Longman III, *The Cry of the Soul* (Colorado Springs: NavPress, 1994), 213.

5. C. S. Lewis, *Letters of C. S. Lewis*, ed. W. H. Lewis (New York: Harcourt, 1966, 1988), 383.

6. Charles Spurgeon, *Gleanings among the Sheaves* (Philadelphia: Lumen Classics, 1864), 44.

7. George M. Marsden, *Jonathan Edwards: A Life* (New Haven, CT: Yale Univ. Press, 2003), 77.

8. Eugene H. Peterson, *Answering God* (San Francisco: HarperSanFrancisco, 1989), 23.

9. Henri J. M. Nouwen, *The Return of the Prodigal Son* (New York: Image Books, 1992), 47.

10. Dietrich Bonhoeffer, *Psalms: The Prayer Book of the Bible* (Minneapolis: Augsburg, 1970), 15.

11. Peterson, *Answering God*, 5.

12. Thomas Merton, *No Man Is an Island* (Boston: Shambhala, 2005), 213.

13. Tim Keller, *The Songs of Jesus* (New York: Viking, 2015), vii.

14. Ibid., viii.

15. Peterson, *Answering God*, 5.

16. Jon Bloom, *Things Not Seen: A Fresh Look at Old Stories of Trusting God's Promises* (Wheaton, IL: Crossway, 2015), 186.

Every Bitter Thing Is Sweet

Tasting the Goodness of God in All Things

Sara Hagerty

Taste the Goodness of God in All Things

Sara Hagerty found Him when life stopped working for her. She found Him when she was a young adult mired in spiritual busyness and when she was a newlywed bride with doubts about whether her fledgling marriage would survive. She found Him alone in the night as she cradled her longing for babies who did not come. She found Him as she kissed the faces of children on another continent who had lived years without a mommy's touch.

In *Every Bitter Thing Is Sweet*, Hagerty weaves fabric from the narrative of her life into the mosaic of a Creator who mends broken stories. Here you will see a God who is present in every changing circumstance. Most significant, you see a God who is present in every unchanging circumstance as well.

Whatever lost expectations you are facing—in family, career, singleness, or marriage—*Every Bitter Thing Is Sweet* will bring you closer to a God who longs for you to know Him more.

Going beyond the narrative to offer timeless insight, Hagerty brings you back to hope, back to healing, back to a place that God is holding for you alone—a place where the unseen is more real than what the eye can perceive. A place where every bitter thing is sweet.

Printed in the USA
CPSIA information can be obtained
at www.ICGtesting.com
JSHW031702150424
61194JS00011B/236

9 780310 358374